The Guru in Your Golf Swing

A golf pro, a monk and the magical Kingdom of Bhutan

To Jennifer,

Ed Hanczaryk

May you uncover the guru
in *your* golf swing!

Ed Hanczaryk
Cape Breton
Fall, 2019

SSP
Publications

SSP Publications recognizes the support of the Province of Nova Scotia. We are pleased to work in partnership with the Department of Communities, Culture and Heritage to develop and promote our cultural resources for all Nova Scotians.

NOVA SCOTIA

Design: Gwen North
All photos: Donna Peacock Hanczaryk, unless otherwise noted

Library and Archives Canada Cataloguing in Publication

Title: The guru in your golf swing : a golf pro, a monk and the magical Kingdom of Bhutan / Ed Hanczaryk.
Names: Hanczaryk, Ed, 1948- author.
Description: Includes bibliographical references.
Identifiers: Canadiana 20190087161 | ISBN 9781989347010 (softcover)
Subjects: LCSH: Hanczaryk, Ed, 1948-—Travel—Bhutan. | LCSH: Golf—Coaching—Bhutan. | LCSH: Buddhist monks—Bhutan. | LCSH: Bhutan—Social life and customs. | LCSH: Bhutan—Description and travel.
Classification: LCC DS491.5 .H36 2019 | DDC 954.98—dc23

E-book ISBN 9781989347027
BISAC OCC010000 SPO016000 TRV003030 TRV026080

Box 2472, Halifax, N.S. B3J 3E4 Canada
www.sspub.ca
sspub@hotmail.com

Printed in Canada

In the Spirit of the Game

Young Bhutanese golfer, hitting a rock with a stick.

"Ed has been essential to the development of countless golfers; myself included. His holistic approach is beneficial for any player, especially aspiring juniors. A balance of swing mechanics, course management and mental clarity are focal points of his instruction. I was able to achieve many of my goals as an elite junior player due to his guidance. Ed's knowledge is vast and wisdom is endless. If you want to improve your game, Ed is the answer."
—Eric Banks, PGA McKenzie Tour

"Ed has done more for me than I ever could have dreamed of. He has pushed me, inspired me allowed me to grow as a golfer, but more importantly as an individual. He is my role model."
—Ally Tidcombe, PGA Tour Latin America

Acknowledgements

Many thanks to many people for encouragement and support. To the people who kept asking "How's it coming?", James and Sharon Hoagland, Mimi McLorie, Meme Coker, John (my conscience) Lawler, Laurie and Landy Mallery, Henry Brunton.

To SSP Publications for taking it on, Bob and Cathy Cosby for use of the Cape Breton cottage, Patti Golden for giving great advice. To Barry Boyce for support and much advice through the years. To Karma Lam, my Bhutanese Brother. To Andrew Holecek for introducing me to dream yoga and for being a great golf partner.

To Katie Hanczaryk for being the world's best daughter and accompanying me to The Kingdom, to Nathan Torti and David Whitehorn for early reading and great feedback. To Liza Matthews for a wonderful cover concept and design.

To Dr. Joe Parent for breaking the ground with Zen Golf and for bringing meditation to the masses of golfers, as well as to the PGA Tour.........and for being a great friend. To the finest golf teacher I have ever known, my mentor in teaching the game, Norrie Wright.

To my editor Kelle Walsh. We never met in person, but I feel like I've known you a long time. To *The Golf News* magazine and Ron Hanna for giving me a monthly writing deadline for 20 summers.

To all the honourable members of the Shambhala Golfers Association and to all you Buddhist golfers with a B name.

To my Buddhist teachers, thank you 108,000 times.

To the love of my life, Donna Lee Peacock Hanczaryk – not only for great photography of the events in Bhutan, but for constant encouragement and friendship.

But without my beloved students in Boulder, Jacksonville, Nova Scotia and Bhutan, this book would not have happened.

Table of Contents

FOREWORD

This book combines the ancient art of meditation with the game of golf: it is a golf fable based on my assignment teaching the game of golf in Bhutan in 2007.

I am a golf professional of 40 years, named one of the top 50 in Canada. I also taught in the US, most notably at Sawgrass Country Club, home of the TPC until 1981. But my most memorable time in golf happened not in North America but in the Himalayan Buddhist Kingdom of Bhutan, where I was invited to teach at the most remote golf course in the world.

There I met a venerable Buddhist Lama, an incarnation of a bygone saint, a renowned teacher of ancient meditation techniques – and a man who was eager to learn how to play golf.

We struck a deal. I would teach him to play the game. He would teach me to meditate, to tame my unruly mind. There, in the soaring mountains, we began our journey.

The golf instruction chapters distill the process that I have seen over 40 years of teaching and tens of thousands of students, of how a swing naturally evolves. The monk did it in five months because of his incredible mental skills. I believe golfers of all levels can benefit from this section.

The meditation chapters present a practice that has been proven by thousands of scientific studies – to increase concentration, improve health and happiness, and to instill a deeper level of calmness in the practitioner.

If one person begins and continues to meditate after reading this book, I will consider it a success. If ten people establish a daily meditation practice, it will be, to me, a bestseller.

INTRODUCTION
GETTING THERE

When it comes to hitting a golf ball, some people have it and some don't.

I had it. And then I lost it.

It took an extended teaching assignment in the hidden Kingdom of Bhutan, high in the Himalayan Mountains and a teenage Buddhist monk to get me back on track. In the process, I trained my unruly mind. This is based on a true story.

Discovering golf

I remember the day, in fact the moment, I got hooked on golf. It was in Amherst, Massachusetts on a summer day; I was an eight-year-old, caddying for my Uncle John. It was the first time I had ever set foot upon a golf course, although I had been whacking a ball around the back forty of Grandpa's farm since I could walk.

My job on that first hole was learning where to stand, where to walk, and what (not) to say. I put clubs back in the bag, held the flag and generally kept out of the way. The problem was, I couldn't see the ball in flight, as John was a good player, literally hitting it out of sight to my untrained eye.

The second tee on that Amherst course is elevated, the green waiting 300 yards below, guarded by water. I happened to be standing directly behind Uncle, as he tried to drive one over the hazard. I still remember the sound, 50 some years later. Persimmon compressing balata (a driver hitting a golf ball) is a sound that stays with you a long time.

But what a sight! The ball took off like nothing I had ever seen, climbing, floating, drifting, seemingly a dot painted in the sky. I must have been quite a vision too, mouth hanging open, my mind ejected into space along with that Spaulding Dot ball. In hindsight, I also glimpsed in that moment that there were other states-of-mind than the one I had become accustomed to. I would, from that point on, aspire to recreating that flight, both of ball and mind.

At that early age, golf was just a cool thing to do. Just five years later, I would latch onto golf to escape what I believed to be a cold, scary world.

I lived a storybook childhood in a rural yet hip part of the world – Amherst, Massachusetts. Hip because of two universities located there, not far from the birthplace of Transcendentalism. Long walks and bike rides in the country-side, exploring the woods with friends, playing baseball – my life was great. But it was about to change, and along with it, my worldview that things were basically good.

Standing in the kitchen one morning with our view of the hills beyond, I recall my parents asking my thoughts of moving to Washington DC. I don't recall what I said, but I do remember the feeling: a deep, bleak sadness.

I found DC rough, raw, urban and not at all friendly or safe. No one looked happy, there were no long walks or even friends. At the tender age of 13, I suddenly felt very alone. That aloneness produced a deep belief that things were not OK, that the world was a hard place.

I did everything I could to escape that sadness, eventually covering it over with an obsession with golf. On the golf course I felt safe.

I began to nag my parents to take me to the course, and every birthday and Christmas asked for golf equipment. I began to play every chance I got. My younger brother Paul got the golf bug at the same time. And so we played, and played, and played. All my friends were now golfers.

Every day I would walk a few miles after school, with a 5-iron and as many balls as I could scrounge up, to the local cemetery.

Two graves were located about 150 yards apart, in a separate field that was unattended by the grounds crew. My quest was to hit the ball from grave to grave, and I remember vividly the day I succeeded in hitting up and back those 150 yards.

Funeral processions often came through while I practiced. When a burial was close enough, I could see people crying as the casket was lowered into the earth. Except for our cat Nini, this was my first notion of death. There were hundreds of graves around me, and it finally dawned on me that my two targets marked what were once living, active people, with loved ones who cried at their funerals.

I began to view my practice range as a sacred ground. My offering to Reverend Albert Watts and Ellie Franklin, the names of the departed on the gravestones, was to aim slightly to the side. For me the perfect shot was to land on the upper slope, with the ball taking a hop over the grave, and settling a few yards below. I also took care to never step directly on the graves, these final resting places.

As I practiced, I often wondered about their lives, where they lived, how they died. The graveyard sessions became a time of contemplation along with the activity of hitting balls.

Back then every opportunity to play golf was magical. One good drive, a long putt, a gimmee birdie – any one of those constituted a good day. Two or three was a memorable one. Every shot offered the potential for magic. Ten bad ones in a row could be erased by one beauty.

Two years after moving to DC, my father took our family with him on a business trip to Chicago, in the dead of winter. At this point I was obsessed with the game, and was having a 'golf jones', withdrawal. In the lobby of the hotel I saw a small sign that read GOLF LESSONS. That evening I found myself in a small room in a nearby warehouse barely high enough to swing, hung with nets.

What happened next was a rare kind of mind-to-mind transmission, pure transfer of knowledge. The teacher was not much taller than me, sharply dressed, charismatic. He told me he was a disciple of golfing legend Ben Hogan, and had a well-worn copy of Hogan's book *The Modern Fundamentals* on a table. We referred to it often during the session.

He taught me to turn my hips to begin the downswing. It was nothing special as far as instruction goes, but it was the first time I had heard of it. On the very first swing I noticed the difference as I moved through the sequence, hips and torso starting, taking all the slack out of my swing, left arm pressed against my chest, flinging the club into the ball. Contact was sweet, the ball felt light. It was the most beautiful thing I had ever felt, and I wanted more.

From that point on, my game developed quickly. The next summer when I was 15, I practiced like a maniac and started to learn to score and compete in junior events. It didn't occur to me that I was playing to escape something.

By age 17 I began to win some local amateur events, attracting the attention of the golf coach at the University of Maryland, who offered me a golf scholarship.

When it came apart

It was in my sophomore year at University of Maryland that I hit the brick wall. It was at a US Open qualifying event at a course in Maryland, competing against a few tour professionals in the field. The day before with my team-mates I was easily under par, hitting every green in regulation. It was the kind of practice round you want – my swing felt good, it was easy, comfortable.

During the practice round I felt like I had back in those magical summer days playing with my brother on the local municipal course. Every shot was an opportunity for wonder. Rather than playing a golf swing, I was playing the course, and it was a tough one.

It was as if the course was communicating with me. Score had nothing to do with it. It was as if the course was presenting a challenge, daring me to hit the only shot for that situation. And shot after shot I responded, no fear and no ego.

I looked forward to carrying that beautiful feeling to the event, and for a short time I did. Two beautifully struck shots on the first left me 15 feet away, straight uphill. My brother Paul was on the bag. Together we read it as a straight uphill putt, a green light.

I went through my routine as always, but I was unable to move the put-ter. I froze. I noticed a puzzled look on my brother's face as I stepped away. I moved back through the routine, and again, I froze. I had the thought that I would stand there all day unless I did something drastic. Jerking the putter away from the ball, I twitched it back, hitting the ground a good three inches before the ball. The putter bounced into the ball, moving it only a few feet. I had to replace the divot.

Again, I addressed the ball, and again the feeling of panic. This time I crashed into it, sending it five feet by. Three putts from there gave me a seven on a hole that I could well have birdied. The same thing happened on the second hole, and my mind left my body. I was in shock. By the fifth hole I was putting with my 5-iron, more a chip than a putt.

The putting yips bled into my full swing and I limped into the clubhouse with a 93, 23 shots higher than the day before.

I lost interest in golf on that day. I quit the golf team, losing what was left of my scholarship. In fact, I stopped playing altogether for a few years, work-ing odd jobs and wondering what to do next. But my deep love of the game, that feeling I got with Uncle John and the pro in Chicago, was too strong. In 1979 I took a job at a course in Maryland, Laurel Pines, and turned pro. I had been away from the game long enough where the scars had healed, and in casual rounds I could still play at a fairly high level.

As an apprentice professional, you are in a competitive dead zone. You can't play in amateur events, and not yet a full PGA member eligible for local pro events. It had been many years since I had competed in a tournament.

However, to gain full membership to the PGA, an apprentice is required to pass a playing test. Nothing spectacular, average 76 over 2 rounds, all in one day, and you're in.

I was 4 under after the first 15 holes, and then that awful feeling came back. I three putted the last three holes for a score of 71, still the low round of the morning but during lunch I didn't talk much. In the afternoon the yips came and went, and I limped in with an 81, to just hit the number. It would be my last competitive round for a very long time.

Becoming a teacher

Three players on the Maryland team went on to play the Tour. I'd proven to myself and everybody else that I wouldn't be one of those competitors. But in order to keep golf in my life, I got a job at a golf course as an assistant professional. I also met a beautiful southern belle, Donna, who would be my wife.

Over the next six years I worked at several clubs in Maryland; at every course I seemed to become the go-to teacher, either because the other pros weren't into it, or simply because I had a knack for it. Then I was offered a coveted job – teaching professional, at Columbia Country Club under one of the all-time great professionals, Bill Strausbaugh.

Bill was an awesome influence, a gifted teacher who pushed me to be the best I could be. Bill had a taste for adventure – something else he would share with me. One

"If you're going through hell, keep going."
— Winston Churchill

13

late afternoon, after a day of teaching, he asked me to consider something: "Ed, fall is here, and the lessons and play will be reduced to almost nothing, he said. There is a teaching job open over the winter at a place I have always wanted to visit, the Kingdom of Bhutan. I am too old to travel that far, and as well I'll need to stay here to take care of business. Why don't you go? All expenses are paid, and Donna would also be invited."

Bhutan? I had never been out of the US. It piqued my interest but sounded far-fetched. Do they even play golf there? What's the weather like? At home that evening I told Donna, and we found the tiny Kingdom on a map. It was on the other side of the world from Maryland, high in the Himalayan Mountains, near Mount Everest. It was a tiny dot, between Tibet and India. We looked at each other and started laughing.

I applied the next day and shortly after that got a call from Rick Lipsey, a *Sports Illustrated* writer and organizer of the Bhutan Youth Golf Association program. Mr. Lipsey celebrated his honeymoon in Bhutan and five years later went back on a *Sports Illustrated* assignment. While in Bhutan, he started the Bhutan Youth Golf Association, an organization that provided daily clinics, tournaments, field trips and scholarships to Bhutanese boys and girls.

I was the fourth or fifth PGA professional who had the assignment to run the program, with the help of the Bhutanese organizer, Karma Lam and Mr. Lipsey.

With Donna's blessing and knowing she would visit for most of the trip, I was off to Asia.

A journey into the unknown

I had never been on a plane for more than three hours and the farthest I had traveled at this point in my life was from Washington to Chicago. My trip to Thimpu, the capital of Bhutan and where I'd be staying for the next five months, took place over 7 days.

It sent me through Hong Kong and then Bangkok, where I watched 2006 turn into 2007 (complete with a terrorist attack on the city that left two people dead and dozens wounded). It was a surreal introduction to what would prove to be an even more surreal experience once I finally arrived at my destination.

But before I arrived in Bhutan I had another 6 hours of travel before me. And I got my first lessons in letting go of notions of how things are 'supposed' to be done (the first of what would be many). In Calcutta my bags were rifled through and clothing stolen. I learned that politely getting into line did not translate. I gave up on personal space and had to simply go with the flow.

The latter stages of the flight turned out to be the most spectacular half hour of visual feasting – the highest range of mountains on our great earth were beneath me and beside me, a view I will never forget. Paro is in a valley, so the plane had to dive steeply once it passed over the last peak, into the fertile flat between the ranges. I saw miles of rice and other crops, in neat but non-linear patches. Many were carved out of the sides of hills, added agricultural space.

I stepped off the plane and was hit by a smell that was almost overpowering. I had to stop and take it in – fresh air from the roof of the earth. I looked around and saw people crying, so overjoyed to be home.

View of Mount Everest from the plane.

MONTH ONE

Discovering Bhutan

The 700,000 or so citizens of Bhutan are fiercely proud of their land. With an area the size of Switzerland, it is guarded on the north by the world's highest range of mountains. In the south is a formidable jungle. It is a monarchy that has never been conquered or colonized, and whose culture has evolved without too much influence from the outside world, until recently.

Buddhism was introduced as early as the second century, but it was in AD 746 that the great Tibetan teacher Guru Rinpoche, also known as *Padmasambhava*, came on the invitation of the King. That much is true, the rest is mythology. As the story goes, there was a powerful demon terrorizing the country that could only be exorcised by a more powerful enlightened being. Guru Rinpoche flew in on a tiger, (to the cave at Taktsang) turning the demon into a rock, and along the way converted the King and the entire country to Buddhism as well. The demon/rock can still be seen on the hike up to the Taktsang Monastery, the most revered in the Kingdom. I made the trek twice while in Bhutan.

The land is dotted with *chortens*, or *stupas* – structures that represent the enlightened mind. The chorten is a large white structure with one golden steeple crowning it and a smaller golden cone above the front porch. It is approached through a small garden and a gate decorated with three slate carvings, representing three protectors. There are rooms inside full of statues and relics. Outside, people pray, meditate, circle it on foot and just hang out and absorb the spiritual vibe that I found palpable.

There are 450 *dzongs*, or monasteries, where an estimated 12,000 monks train in the ancient practices of meditation and contemplation. Even in downtown Thimphu you can't go far before seeing a monk in maroon robes, perhaps on break from the rigors of the monastery.

A chorten.

Oddly, at least half of the monks I saw wore red Nike hats. I wondered: Could it be that Nike is also sponsoring students of the enlightened mind? The mystery was solved when I walked into a shop advertising everything a robed monk would need, and more. Lined up next to the robes, beads and prayer wheels, were rows and rows of Nike 'swoops', on warm red caps.

At the time, Thimpu was the only capital city with no stoplights. I watched mesmerized as a policeman directed traffic using elegant arm motions that reminded me of tai chi.

It took me a week to begin to acclimatize myself to the altitude of 7400 feet, the food and how to get around. Everything moves slowly in Bhutan, including the internet, which had only reached The Kingdom a few years before I arrived. Thanks to the altitude, even the water takes forever to boil. And I quickly learned a few important rules; don't talk about the King in public and don't point.

Teaching at the Indian Embassy.

I also learned what the world's highest mountain range produces in a small country. Over the next hill, there was another language, two mountain ranges over, still another. And they are different enough to be not understood by each other. When I went into a bank to make change, the cashier reached into her pocketbook! There were no cash registers that I could see. Even the grocery store only had a cash drawer.

The athletes of Thimphu – natural golfers

After a week exploring the capital, I began to carry out the mission to introduce the game of golf to juniors from age 8 to 17, living in the capital city of Bhutan. The training would be held at Royal Thimpu Golf Club, described in one article as "The Most Remote Course in the World." Surrounded by dramatic mountains, it is a spectacular sight. It's important to keep it in the fairway; hitting it off line into the jungle here is literal.

I was to teach five days a week, to a group of up to 40 students. There was no typical student. One boy might have been a member of the royal family, while another boy slept in a hut. I was also encouraged to take them on field

Bhutanese youth.

trips, and I would make trips to schools in remote regions of the country. The only day we really had full use of the course was on Mondays, when it was otherwise closed. The rest of the week we were relegated to a small rectangular patch of mostly bare dirt.

I taught a bit at the Indian Embassy in Bhutan, the only embassy in the world with its own golf course. All the golfers in Bhutan are amateurs, yet the big tournament of the year, played at the Embassy, offers a car as first prize (I learned a year later that one of my junior students won it after I left). Handicaps in Bhutan are strictly tournament scores, not based on every day play – not a bad idea!

Bhutan – a small country with a culture of sportsmanship

I have found that good golfers have a background in many sports.

One weekend as I strolled through the capital, around me were pick-up sporting events – kids walking down the street keeping a soccer ball in the air with their feet, others chucking rocks at a tree. Further down the road I came upon a group of about 30 men, dressed in traditional *gho*, the national outfit, throwing home-made, torpedo-looking darts a good 30 yards, to a target about two feet wide by three feet high. And, to my amazement, hitting it frequently.

Archery target, called a *buh*.

I stopped alongside 30 or so other spectators to watch the action.

One of the contestants saw me doing my Tom Brady impression up in the bleachers, pretending to throw a football. He invited me down to try. It'd been a few years since I tried to throw a football for any distance, but I used to have a pretty good arm.

The dart was a sharpened iron rod, about 2 feet long, with feathers. The handle was just a rounded piece of wood.

I did a few stretches, wound up and fired. The dart fell five yards to the left of the target and a good 15 yards short. Second toss, the same result. The players and spectators all got a good laugh at my expense. I stuck around a few minutes longer to watch the 'pros' and was astounded at their strength and accuracy as two direct hits sailed by, followed by a little song and dance by the winning team.

As fun as it is to watch *khuru*, the national sport in Bhutan is archery. It doesn't seem possible that they could hit the target from the distances they are shooting from – 150 yards. And there are the distractions around the game. People are dancing and yelling and standing dangerously close to the target being shot at. Their focus is inspiring, and the juniors seem to have it naturally.

During my time in Bhutan I gave a golf lesson to a businessman who had been one of the best archers in the country. He took up the game eight months prior with a passion, quitting archery because he felt golf produced more camaraderie amongst competitors. (When he told me this I remembered that golf was once banned in Scotland because it detracted from archery practice, which in turn supposedly weakened the military.)

He had a wicked slice and the harder he hit it, the more it would curve to the right. A little grip change, a little forearm rotation through impact, and he was soon hitting it well. Once his gun started shooting straight, he could now use those super aiming powers learned in archery. The ball shag boy was catching most of his drives after one bounce, without having to move much. (No range ball pickers here. The caddies and shag boys were all in the junior program.)

The children don't have store bought toys; instead they have many games with rocks. I saw some boys playing a rock toss game for hours, and girls playing a game with pebbles – throwing them up, catching them on the backs of their hands, then tossing them up again and catching what's left with their palms up. The one with the most rocks after a series of tosses was the winner.

In addition to being good athletes, they were all math whizzes. They were way faster than me in adding things mentally. I never found an explanation for that. Maybe there were some super math teachers in the schools. When we played, they all kept track of everybody's scores and who was up in matches, without a scorecard.

Blending golf with archery – a new sport is born

The professionals working with the Bhutan Youth Golf Association are assigned for three to five-month periods. Mine was a five-month mission. The pros were all well known in town – word travels quickly here. They are in some ways understood as the next incarnate 'golf lama'.

On my first day of teaching, Karma Lam, my Bhutanese counterpart with the program, picked me up at my apartment in Thimpu and we arrived at the course just outside of town at 9:30 am. There were 24 juniors aged 9 to 16 there, chipping around and waiting. Very few had their own clubs, but enough clubs and balls are provided by the program where they each have at least one to use. A lot of sharing takes place.

As Lam assembled the group, I couldn't believe the beauty surrounding me. Mountains up to 24,000 feet surrounded this little valley, and I felt like I was looking almost straight up, straining my neck to see the top. I could see dzongs all over, many near the peaks. Many of these monasteries are centuries old.

The class began with three children coming out one at a time to sing songs. Their voices were beautiful and as they sang, we all clapped in time. Two of the songs were in the local language, which is song-like even in normal conversation. The other song was in English, about life in the army!

Lam, who was trained as a European Level 2 coach and served on the Bhutanese Olympic committee, led the group in a warm-up, aided by one of the older students. We then made our way down to the practice area where the kids paired up to work on chipping, hitting two balls each, then changing places.

We did this for a while, but the juniors soon grew bored. Thinking about an archery match I'd watched the day before, I had an idea:

I had brought boxes of Red Hots (candy) with me from Maryland as prizes

A rousing game of Golchery.

for the kids, after learning that chilies are part of every Bhutanese meal. As before, they chipped to each other, but this time there was both a target and a prize. If the ball knocked down the box, the golfer got to eat one Red Hot.

Boy did that change their focus! It took a while to get the range, but I saw some chipping that would hold up against even experienced golfers. One young fellow, the only lefty, hit a box nine times! (It was only after practice that I discovered the candy itself wasn't the big draw. I asked one of the girls, Tashi, if she enjoyed the candy. She made a sour face and replied that it tasted like medicine!)

That night, I went around to some shops, collecting cardboard that I would make into buhs. I must have been a strange site – a Caucasian man rummaging through the recycle trash heaps, with large pieces of cardboard under his arm. One shop proprietor thought I was selling the cardboard and kindly told me that he had enough!

Back at my apartment, using duct tape I had thankfully brought with me, I made two buh-targets with the same markings as on the buh the adults used in archery.

During the next class, I set up the targets about 50 yards apart. I split the kids into teams, the Tigers vs the Snow Lions, and each team took turns to try and hit the target. A team earned one point for a hit, two if the target was knocked down. The kids took to 'Golchery' immediately.

In my life of competitive sports, I had never seen a closer or more exciting contest. After the first round, there was only one point scored. An 18 inch by three-foot target from 50 yards, off of bare dirt, is not exactly a gimmie.

But in round two, points began adding up. When Tashi of the Snow Lion team came up, the score was 5 to 4. She took dead aim and knocked the buh over, putting her team ahead 6 to 5. Last up was Rinchen, the best player of the group, a young man who lives in a small hut next to the course.

With eyes narrowed and focus like the raven (the Bhutanese national bird), he hit a low stinger, banging the buh straight on. It teetered and then fell, for a last-minute victory. Doug Flutie's famous Hail Mary pass in college football putting Boston College over the University of Miami was no more exciting.

Unjaded junior golfers

When we went out to play the course on Monday, each player got one ball, and one or two clubs that were shared among the group. There was a driver, fairway metal, mid and short iron and putter for each foursome. The driver might have had a loft of 8.5 with a stiff, cut-off shaft, which made it even stiffer. Compare this to our young guys and girls in North America, with the latest, often fitted, equipment.

If the ball was lost, that's game over. But these kids have keen eyes, and except for in water, could usually find the ball. (Many of them also caddy at the course to help with the family living expenses.) But one of the hardest things I have ever had to say was: "you can't play anymore, there are no balls."

And boy, these Bhutanese youth could play! They had never received the well-intended but ill-advised instructions of 'keeping your head down' and 'stiffen that left arm'. There was also little of the no-turn, pick-the-club-up-with-the-arms movement so common in North America. The only golf coaching they'd ever had was from a professional working with the Association.

They had learned to play on bare dirt. The only way to hit a golf ball with any kind of success was to pinch it or squeeze it off the ground. No scoopers here. Unlike some of our lush, forgiving fairways, here a molecule off meant a bad shot. They learned on their own and from each other, out of necessity, to reach impact with a forward leaning shaft.

They also had wonderful rhythm, simply because they weren't thinking about it. Back home, it's so common to see painfully slow backswings – another misguided instruction to try to hit the ball further. Distance comes from club head speed and that means higher, not lower. These kids knew that organically.

The monastery

A few weeks into the assignment Karma Lam told me that the Tango Goemba Buddhist Monastery outside of town contacted him, asking that the new golf pro in town come out to teach. It seems that the head of the monastery, an 18-year-old with students all over the world, made the request.

We couldn't drive, as the monastery rests on the side of Cheri mountain. Just a few miles as the raven flies, the trek on foot – carrying all the clubs, balls and other gear – took our small party an hour, as the trail narrowed into a footpath. I was worn out when I reached the pass, not used to the altitude. During the trek, several elders zipped past our little party with huge bundles of sticks strapped to their backs – fuel for the monastery kitchen.

The view from the top took my breath away. Row after row of mountain ranges were visible in the distance. Large birds floated on the wind currents – Himalayan Vultures, Golden Eagles, Crested Honey Buzzards, Bat Hawks. The dzong itself was a series of classic square Bhutanese buildings with raised roofs for ventilation. Behind it was a large field, closely mown. I found out later the yaks took care of the greens-keeping duties, much like the sheep in the old days at St. Andrews in Scotland.

We set up the cardboard buh I had made for the kids and I waited as 20 or so young monks, all wearing maroon robes, gathered around our makeshift tee. I started my typical first group clinic, when Lam stopped me: "Ed, these boys don't speak English, only Dzongkha, the local dialect."

Cheri Monastery.

So, I had to teach without speaking! It turned out to be the best introductory lesson I ever gave. I demonstrated the athletic golf stance, using the few words I had learned from my juniors in the Thimphu class. Of course, they first taught me the naughty words; 'Abu up!' I proclaimed when teaching the stance. Abu is Dzongkha for 'rear end'.

To teach the proper grip I made my hands into a gesture of two bird wings, with a little pressure where the bottom of the thumb touches the palm of the hand. I put a tee in that place of pressure. I then showed how the hands fit on the club, with the tee lining up on the top of the handle.

Then, beginning with a short chip shot, I demonstrated how the shaft leans slightly forward at impact. I hit a few shots, forward leaning shaft, with the club just skimming the ground. The best chippers have a shallow arc.

The monks all knew Bhutanese archery, so the buh and the scoring system were familiar. They lined up to have a turn. Golchery was a way to teach golf technique in a small space while making it fun.

Many hours of meditation, and lack of modern entertainment distractions like TV and Internet, had formed these young mens' minds into laser beams. They modeled my demonstration nearly perfectly, getting the ball airborne nearly every time.

One monk, addressing the ball with the same raven-eye focus I'd watched a few days earlier, hit his shots through the small circle in the middle of the buh nearly every time, a feat for any golfer but amazing for a raw beginner. He addressed the ball with eyes that narrowed into two slits, eagle-like – a look that I had seen in Rinchen a few days before.

The monks seemed delighted to be there. There was lots of laughter and what I assumed to be Bhutanese trash-talk in Dzongkha going on as they took turns. Lam was chuckling as well and he helped at times with translations. What struck me was how close we were to a sheer cliff, a good 100 feet down. One ball took a sideways bounce and careened over the edge, which evoked a roar of laughter from everybody except me.

After the session the monks went back to meditation practice. I was invited in to one of the buildings where Lam and I were served butter tea made from yak butter and hot red peppers with cheese, called *ema datshi*. One bite of the chili dish and my eyes began to water. (The Bhutanese chili is some of the hottest in the world.)

As we walked back down the mountain, Karma Lam asked me if we could make this a weekly event. I immediately said yes.

Meeting Rinpoche

Tibetan and Bhutanese Buddhists believe that after death you will be suddenly without a body, but part of you continues. Call it energy, or mind, but some part of us moves on through the transition between death and rebirth.

They also believe that people who, while here in human form, have reached a certain level of understanding and are able to choose their rebirth – where and when and who they will be in their next life.

The rest of us, meanwhile, eternally tread on the hamster wheel of *samsara* and are blown around like feathers in the wind.

A Rinpoche is one of those enlightened beings that come back consciously, in order to do good for the sake of all sentient beings.

The head of the monastery that served as my golf academy was a Rinpoche. I found this out well after our first meeting.

It was during the second weekly clinic at my high-in-the-sky driving range on a mountain nearly 12,000 feet high that I noticed a young man watching from the highest window in the dzong. Afterward, as I was in the process of packing up, an older monk approached me: "Rinpoche is inviting you to his suite and would like to meet you."

I found out later that he has students all over the world and in major centers in China, the US, India and Canada. To have a one-on-one meeting was highly unusual, or as the Tibetans would say, auspicious. Rinpoche's room was on the upper floor, not palatial but definitely royal, with rich orange brocade and a beautiful rug with an image of three jewels.

We sat facing each other, he cross-legged on an ornate box and me on a chair. He was very handsome, a well-proportioned, relaxed face. He was 18 years of age but carried himself with a maturity way beyond teenage years.

"Tell me what it takes to be a PGA golf professional. Did you play on the tour?" Right off the get-go, his first question pinpointed my previous failures in the heat of battle.

"Rinpoche, I was good enough physically, but unable to perform when I needed to. My mind got in the way." I was mirroring the words a PhD sports psychologist had told me. Unfortunately, the good doctor didn't show me how to fix it.

"I see…when you most needed your mind to be an ally, it turned on you and became an enemy." Wow, I thought, talk about getting right to the point – no small talk here.

"Ed, I would like to go on a journey with you in the months you have remaining in Bhutan. For two years I studied at Oxford University in England and at the urging of some friends there, I took up the game. I was able to play and practice at the Southfield Golf Club, a guest of a member who was a meditation student of mine. I love the game but have hit a point where I am not improving and would like professional help. My offer is: I can help you to tame your mind, if you will teach me the technique of playing golf."

I didn't hesitate: "Rinpoche, you have a deal."

We shook hands and said goodbye and I left the room. His attendant then

Yogi Berra said it: "Ninety percent of golf is half mental."

took me to the waiting room and we talked about a schedule – a once a week meditation session, then the next day a golf lesson. I teach him and he teaches me, with both of us practicing in between. The first meeting would be the next day, at the golf course.

First golf lesson – attention on the club, not the ball

The young monk was not tall, maybe around the height of Ben Hogan, 5'- 6". He walked onto the tee confidently, surely, almost gliding. One of his students in Thailand knew he played, and generously sent him a set of top-of-the-line Titleist clubs. Looking at the marks on the sole from usage, I knew immediately that they didn't fit him, but they would do for the time being.

Just as he had interviewed me and gotten to the point quickly, I didn't waste time finding out about his athletic and golfing background. His lack of experience was a disadvantage, I thought, but not a deal breaker. He was also a natural right hander.

What he had practiced was archery, which is the Bhutanese national sport. He was highly accomplished at this and had studied extensively with Shabata Sensei, who was the 20th in the lineage of bow makers for the Emperor of Japan. Sensei was the most accomplished teacher and practitioner of Kyudo, or Zen archery, in the world.

The Lama is right handed, so much of the golf instruction speaks to him as such, as a righty. So you lefties will have to switch right with left. My apologies (but you are probably used to it.) Interspersed with right and left hand are the terms *target* and *trail* hand. The target hand is the one closest to the target, trail hand is the one furthest away.

I also found out that Rinpoche was fond of throwing a frisbee, a motion that closely resembles the correct action of the lead arm in a golf swing. All good news, as from archery and frisbee he knew about target orientation, trajectory, tension and load, release, focus.

The caddy put down the shag bag in front of us, and I sent him out around 100 yards. "Sir, here's a 9-iron. Hit a few to the caddy if you will."

The first shot barely moved ten feet, his club digging

into the ground a good eight inches in front of the ball. The second was hit squarely on the hosel, a classic shank.

I got out my little Casio camera and filmed the next two from a couple of angles. A pull hook and finally a semi-solid shot that went no more than 50 yards, high right. We had a lot of work to do.

The video confirmed what my eyes saw – in the backswing his upper body moved a good foot to the left, toward the target. Coming down, his hands went out nearly horizontally, then sharply down. The angle between his arms and the club released way too soon, a classic scoop. And throughout the whole process his clubface was open a good 45 degrees from square. This was a swing I had seen thousands of times before. It took commitment and a great deal of body awareness to get this player to playing decent golf.

"Sir, in your past golfing experience have you ever had any instruction?"

"Not formally, but I played with some pretty good golfers who gave me lots of tips."

"And what did they tell you?" I asked.

"Well, for the grip, put your thumbs on top of the handle, keep your head down, watch the ball and don't look up."

Right there, I thought, at the very beginning of a golfer's career, bad instruction had set the stage for a lifetime of bad golf unless there was an intervention from a PGA pro. His well-meaning friends had passed along what someone had told them, the way a dangerous virus is passed from person to person.

The path I needed to lead him down became clear. This would obviously be a building process, rather than a fixing procedure. Sometimes in golf instruction, fixing is fine, but with my young student that would be like putting band-aids on top of band-aids, temporary at best. Plus, I knew I had him for the long haul.

One is not polishing one's shooting style or technique, but the mind. The dignity of shooting is the important point. This is how Kyudo differs from the common approach to archery. In Kyudo there is no hope. Hope is not the point. The point is that through long and genuine practice your natural dignity as a human being comes out. This natural dignity is already in you, but it is covered up by a lot of obstacles. When they are cleared away, your natural dignity is allowed to shine forth.
—Kanjuro Shibata

"Good golf begins with a good grip."
—Ben Hogan, Arnold Palmer, Tiger Woods

I had to do this systematically, with one step building on another. Step one had to be to replace the ball focus with target focus. His reverse pivot backswing, the steep downswing, the early release – all originated with thinking the wrong thoughts, head down being the worst.

First was a small adjustment on his stance. In trying to keep his head down, his usually straight spine was bowed. The notion of 'head down' is like a fruit fly to a peach, it mysteriously appears. Facing him, all I could see was the top of his head. I used the term 'abu up' to get him in a more athletic posture, armpits over balls of feet. He picked it up immediately.

Next, I had to deal with the problem of where one should pay attention when hitting a golf ball.

"Sir, when you shoot an arrow, what are you thinking about?"

He answered: "I am connecting a sense of my body, poised and stretched, the target and the space in between."

"Well begun is nearly done."
—Bill Strausbaugh, my first coach

"Rinpoche, how do you think you would perform if you only thought about the arrow? The bow shoots the arrow and you control the bow. Rest your eyes on the ball, but don't think about it. Swing the club, brushing the ground."

He smiled at me. He got it.

I had him hit a few more, changing his focus from ball to club. His swing immediately looked freer and the swing speed audibly went up. The contact improved and the bottom of the arc moved left, closer to the ball.

The weak, high right shot that resulted was another matter, for another day.

Golf lesson review:

- Athletic stance; no 'head down.'
- Change of attention from ball to club, specifically for newer golfers, where it brushes the ground.

Meditation session – feeling your body

I woke up early the next day, excited and yet very unsure about what to expect. It was my turn to be the student. While waiting in the outer chamber, my mind raced. I pictured him teaching me how to meditate, how to quiet my mind. I saw myself becoming calmer, oblivious to worry and stress. I was sure this would help my golf game.

His attendant woke me from my reverie: "Rinpoche will see you now."

As before we sat facing each other, he cross-legged on an ornate throne, me on a chair.

"So Ed, why do you think you choke?" His directness caught me off guard, even though it was not the first time he had done so.

"Sir, I seem to lose the flow of my normal game when the chips are down. Nothing seems to work and I get into this awful state of mind that I would call frantic. The more I try to stop the negative thoughts, the worse it gets."

He thought about that for a minute, then asked: "So how is that different from those times you play well, your normal round?"

"When I play well, I am fully engaged in the game. Nothing bothers me, a bad shot is only one shot, the next is usually better. The club feels a certain way in my hands, while when I am off, I can't even feel it."

Again, a pause, then he spoke in a measured, quiet voice:

"Ed, you showed me yesterday that I needed to pay attention to something else, other than the ball. I would ask you to also pay attention to something different. Your attention and where it is directed is your greatest weapon against an unruly mind."

"Sit with me for a while – straight back, upright head and shoulders. Sound familiar? You taught me that in our golf session. Your spine will feel strong and erect, but your chest

> "We are what we think. All that we are arises with our thoughts. With our thoughts we make the world."
> —Buddha, *The Dhammapada*

31

will feel open, soft. Keep your eyes open and let them rest on the floor, five or six feet out. Don't stare, rest your gaze there." He winked at me…he used the same words I used yesterday.

"Now, let's sit here a few minutes, just feeling the points of contact, rear end on the chair, feet on the ground, hands on thighs."

As we sat in silence, I started fantasizing about the tournaments I would enter when I got home. I saw myself walking confidently to the first tee at the PGA Club Professional event, people noticing my confidence. I was about to hit my tee shot when I was startled by the sound of a gong.

When the sound died down, Rinpoche asked me about our short session, specifically what I thought about during the session.

"Sir, I had some very happy positive thoughts. I was planning some tournaments I have avoided for years."

His smile resembled those on the statues of the Buddha in the ornate shrine room, subtle, the lips turning up ever so slightly on either side of his mouth.

"So, just like my mind was fixated on the ball, yours was attached to an event in the future. You weren't paying attention to the points of contact."

I blushed. If there is a meditation equivalent of a hacker, that would be me. I owned up to it and basically asked for a mulligan.

"Can we try this again? This time I'll try to follow directions!"

Again we sat, and try as I might, points of contact were not as entertaining

---

I took a group of junior students to Florida one winter; by chance we were invited to Sean Foley's teaching facility, Core Golf, in Orlando. During his inspiring talk, he casually mentioned that his most famous former student Tiger Woods is a meditator, as is Foley himself.

After his talk, I raised my hand. "Sean, if you were to get on Google, and type in 'benefits of meditation,' thousands of pages come up." (In fact, the last time I checked there were 21,800 items). "And it is well known that Tiger was trained as a child in Thai Buddhist meditation, going to the temple with his mother. And we know Tiger has a mental edge, his record proves that. So why doesn't every tour player meditate?"

He took a minute to think about his answer. "They don't do it because it's so hard." In my words, it's hard because it seems so easy and because the results are not immediate.

---

as winning golf tournaments in my mind. This time I went as far as holding the trophy! When I realized I was again not following orders, I got mad at myself, angry at my weak mind. The sound of the gong snapped me out of it.

"Where did you go this time?" Rinpoche asked, as if he knew that Elvis had left the building.

"Rinpoche, I guess I am unable to stop my mind, which is exactly what happens on the golf course."

"Ed, here's the main point," he said. "Your mind thinks; that is what it is supposed to do. Your eyes see, your ears hear, your nose smells, and your mind thinks. I am not asking you to get rid of thoughts, because that would be impossible. I am asking you, just as you asked me yesterday, to not give them so much importance. The ball is still there, I'm just not paying attention to it. Don't be bothered by your thoughts, just let them come and go."

"Practice the exercise of paying attention to your body and where you feel it contact your environment, for 24 minutes a day." This was the traditional length of time, called *ghatika*, prescribed to beginners, he told me.

He had one more piece of advice: "If you find you are lost in thoughts, keep coming back to your body."

We were done. I had my homework. "I'll see you next week," he said. "We both need a lot of practice."

> "The people in one study were lost in thought 47% of the time."
> —Andy Puddicombe, *Ted Talk*

Meditation session review:

- Good posture, upright, relaxed.
- Attention to the points of contact.
- When the mind wanders, come back to the points of contact.

Golf lesson – the bottom of the arc

On my 20-minute walk to meet Rinpoche at the Royal Thimpu Golf Club range, I passed a donkey walking down the middle of the street, holding up traffic. The good news was that there were not many cars, at least compared to where I'm from.

I sent the caddy out, but not so far this time. I handed my young student a wedge and told him to take some practice swings to feel the weight of the club. His swing looked better, freer – that was the good news.

The bad news was that, like before, the contact was all over the place. The balls that were not hit fat rolled along the ground. The ones he did hit on the clubface went extremely high and right.

I asked him my stock quiz: "Every circle, unless horizontal, has a low point relative to the ground. Rinpoche, relative to the ball lying there and the caddy as a target, point at the ideal low point."

Like a thousand of my students before him, he pointed at a spot a few inches to the right of the ball.

"So, to get a ball into the air, you have to get under it and lift it, right?" He answered yes. "It is my understanding that if you top a ball you didn't get under it – you lifted your head."

I was waiting in ambush. "Sir, I will ask you to stand facing me as I hit a few shots. Notice where my club hits the ground." My first shot with a 7-iron was as solid as I can hit it and it went off like a bullet, 50 yards over the caddy's head.

"Where did I hit the ground?"

I could see the epiphany in his eyes.

"Your divot was on the target side of the ball, the bottom being a few inches in front! You didn't lift it at all, in fact, just the opposite."

"All right, I want to see a legitimate swing, no scooping."
—Roy McAvoy (a.k.a. Kevin Costner) in *Tin Cup*

We ended lesson two with an explanation and an exercise. I showed him how a forward-leaning shaft is the only way to get the bottom of the arc in the right place when the ball is on the ground. Then I drew a line in the dirt and asked him to – strike the match – to the left of the line.

Then I gave him a 7-iron and asked him to hit a few shots. While the ball flight was still well to the right, a few shots had that unmistakable sound of compression, taking off on a much lower trajectory. *He is turning out to be an exceptional student*, I thought as we parted. Little did I know how exceptional he would be.

Golf lesson review:

- The bottom of the arc for irons is *past* the ball, no 'getting under' it.
- Strike the match – don't lift.

Meditation session – keep coming back to the breath

The next day it was my turn on his turf. I had dutifully done the practice of noticing the points of contact, rear end to chair, hands on thighs, feet on ground – for a half hour each day.

"So, Ed, tell me how your first week of practice went?" he asked in greeting.

"Rinpoche, frankly not very well." I replied honestly. "It's not really working, in fact I'm getting worse. I have way more thoughts now than I did before! What's that about?"

He chuckled. "Truth be known, those thoughts have always been there, you just never noticed them before. Your mind blows around like a feather in the wind. You have reached the first plateau, noticing that our minds churn constantly."

He went on to explain that there are so many obstacles to meditation practice, that the great meditators of the past created a sort of user's manual to identify them: laziness, forgetfulness, drowsiness, wildness and craziness – and carelessness.

At my stage, Rinpoche explained, there are two main obstacles: a dull, heavy mind and an excited mind. The antidote to dullness is belief and faith

"At the beginning, of the practice, your mind will seem like a wild horse, it is too elusive and jittery to even get close enough to ride. But if you begin to ease up to it, giving it a very long lead line, it will begin to relax and get used to you. Maybe you leave it an apple every day, and slowly and very gently shorten the line.

Eventually it will be eating out of your hand."
—the author

in the power of meditation. "At this point you will have to just trust me, but as your practice deepens, you will see what I mean," he said.

It also helps to lift your gaze if you feel dull, he said. Also: "Tighten up your discipline. You are sitting there for 24 minutes to meditate, not to plan the future. Often, we sit just going through the motions" Rinpoche said. "Tighten it up if you are being dull."

The antidote to an excited mind, he continued, is understanding impermanence. "It will pass. Just keep doing the practice. It also helps to feel into your body, into the relaxation – and to shift your gaze downward."

For this meditation session, he asked me to pay attention only to my breath. "It could be your stomach rising and falling, or the breath coming in and out of your nose, or even the sound of breathing. Or, all of those together."

"When your mind invariably wanders to a thought," he said, "the moment you notice it, come back to the breath." And 'thoughts' he explained, include rehashing the past, rehearsing the future, or even experiencing an emotion like anger.

There was just one more step: "When you notice you have wandered away from the attention on the breath, gently say to yourself the word 'thinking,' and then come back to the breathing. Over and over and over again."

"Any questions?" he added.

I did have one. I had downloaded some relaxing music to play while I went to bed in the evening. I asked if I could listen to that while I meditated.

"Ed, no music. This is not a practice of escaping – rather it is a practice of paying attention to your world."

"Wow," I thought, "not an escape?"

We then sat quietly in meditation for a few minutes before he struck the gong. "See you tomorrow at Royal Thimphu, Ed."

Meditation session review:

- Keep your attention now on the breath.
- When you lose attention on the breath, just come back to it.
- When you catch yourself thinking, label it 'thinking'.
- Meditation is not an escape or blank out. You are fully present.

Golf lesson – the club face

It was another balmy day in the Kingdom. I expected it to be cooler, seeing that we were so high. But Bhutan is at the same latitude as Mexico, next to India, and shares the same climate as the east of India.

As I walked to the course from my apartment, I made my lesson plan. Up until this point Rinpoche and I had worked mostly on the concept of what makes the ball do what it does, and the correct understanding of what should happen in the swing, dispelling the false advice he had received in the past. Today I would introduce the nitty gritty of the clubface, which I considered the single most critical element of a good golf swing.

From the bad instruction he had gotten in the past, Rinpoche had developed a club face that was open right from the start. Placing your thumbs on top of the handle makes sense to a novice, but it is one of the causes of slicing, the bane of most golfers.

Rinpoche was waiting for me and the caddy had already assumed his position out on the range. The young monk had been practicing; his freed-up swing looked much more natural, but he was still hitting the high right shots. We reviewed the line-in-the-dirt drill, just as I had with my juniors, and without the ball Rinpoche consistently hit to the left of the line. But having put the ball down he would bottom out early.

I showed him how to bend from the hips, drop the club and let his arms go limp, and had him see how they turn inward quite a bit. Previously, when he picked up the club that natural hang disappeared.

I suggested he should match that natural hanging, relaxed and with some of the back of his hands visible. Instead of thumbs on top, I suggested he place his left thumb slightly to the right and the right thumb slightly to the left.

"I want you to see, while looking down without moving your head, two knuckles and a sliver of the third on each hand." I told him.

He easily made the change. And after a few practice swings, he actually hit a few shots that instead of going high right, went hard left – lower and longer. The caddy was surprised. But he still kept the club too open late in the downswing, a fault that would limit his progress to a mighty degree. His left wrist was cupping, affecting the face. Good for flop shots and sand, but not so good for anything else.

"Sir, I know you like to throw a frisbee. I know you are naturally right handed, but if you were to throw lefty, what would it look like?"

I had found an aluminum pie tin in my apartment and had stuck it into my teaching bag. I pulled it out and handed it to him.

"Now, rear back as if you are going to heave it a long way, then stop and look at your left hand," I said.

He noticed right away that his wrist was slightly bowed. "Now take it back incorrectly, with your left wrist cupped."

Instead of correcting it I asked him to try to throw the tin like that.

He immediately realized that there was no way to throw with any power or control in that manner. "Interesting," he whispered, as he explored the difference between the two positions.

Now I asked him to notice that the palm position of his left hand faced him in the correct position." Take your 7-iron and in little half swings, try to repeat what you just felt," I said. "Try to keep the feeling of your left palm facing you all the way to impact."

He had amazing control of his body and mind. The first shot, with a short, easy swing, flew 20 yards over the caddy's head. In just three sessions, Rinpoche was building a swing that produced a great impact, with the club leaning forward and the bottom of the arc forward of the ball.

A few more weeks of this, I thought, and he'll be ready to play golf, and graduate from the golf swing to playing the game.

Review of golf lesson:

- Understanding the club face and how it is affected by the grip, and specifically the position of the left wrist.

Meditation session – fresh start

Rinpoche looked bigger today on his throne. It's odd how perceptions change. Maybe I was seeing him in a different light. We started the session, as always, with a bow to each other, then I immediately jumped in to share my experience over the week.

"There were a few moments when I was fully with the breath," I told him. "They were short, but I felt like at least I was doing the practice. For the most part, though, I was lost in thought as usual."

He asked me to be specific. Was I thinking about the past, the future? Was my thinking foggy and dull, or wild and excited?

"There was just a constant low-key distraction, like a headache in my mind, not my head," I answered. "For the most part I found myself playing golf in the future. Sometimes I would think about my stay here ending and leaving you. Other times I had a song in my head, something that often would happen on the course. Mostly, I don't know where I went, or for how long."

I was surprised when he answered: "OK, very good. You are on the path to taming your mind."

He said little gaps were occurring, indicating that I was nearing the point where 'taming the mind' becomes 'training the mind.'

My homework was to continue as it had been: sitting with a straight back, soft front body, resting my eyes on a point on the ground in front of me – to start by noticing the points of contact and then moving on to noticing my breath.

"If you find yourself thinking, planning, reminiscing, angry, sad, dull, excited, whatever it is – label it 'thinking' and come back to the breath. The noticing and coming back is the practice," he explained.

He told me that it's not uncommon for beginning meditators to spend

The fact is, with modern MRI technology, it has been proven that meditators' brains get bigger, in the good places, the focus areas, quiet areas, happiness areas, visualization skills, ability to control stress and stay in the moment, and so on.

Meditation has been practiced for over 2500 years; the road is well marked. Like a GPS, an experienced teacher (can be a book by an experienced teacher), will tell you when you have made a wrong turn.
—the author

nearly the entire session lost in thought. Coming back to the breath, he said, is like pushing a reset button.

"Even if you only come back once, it could be a productive session," he said. "There is no such thing as a bad session."

We sat for a few more minutes and then I heard the gong, as if I was hearing it for the first time. I listened deeply without thought, until the sound faded.

"See you tomorrow, Sir. Thanks." I said as I started to get up.

"Ed," he said, "there is a large meadow behind the monastery, kept short by the yaks we keep for milk. Why don't we meet there tomorrow instead of the golf course?"

"Sounds good, Sir. I'll see you at 9."

That night during my weekly Skype call home, my wife said I looked different, my face more relaxed, my voice softer. Interesting, I thought. The last couple of days I had felt different – lighter, happier. I felt more home in my body and tuned into my environment.

Surely part of this had to do with being in this beautiful, relaxed place. But even I could tell that the daily practice of meditation was subtly, but definitely shifting me as well. As my 20 year-old daughter Katie would say, I was being 'chill'.

Review of meditation session:

- Following the breath, when we get lost in thought, just come back to the breath.
- Little gaps between thoughts will start to occur. Notice those gaps.
- There is always a chance for a fresh start.

Golf lesson – staying in motion

The next golf lesson was held at the monastery. The field doubles as grazing for the yaks and archery practice. It was mown beautifully by the big creatures. One of the young monks, Karma, was the ball caddy.

As always I asked Rinpoche to make a few practice swings and I was pleased by the flow in his motion. But when I asked him to hit one, it became jerky. While his swing was miles better than when we started, it was still lacking something.

I realized that the missing ingredient was what's known as a waggle, then forward press. A waggle is a wrist and arm mini-swing before the shot and a forward press is a little movement toward the target to start the move away from the target. He was starting from a dead stop; a flowing motion must have a trigger.

I waved the caddy to come in and I asked him using sign language to go to the nearby stream to fill the now empty ball bucket with water. Five minutes later, I demonstrated to my student a trick I learned from Harvey Penick's *Little Red Book*.

Holding the pail in front of me, with one hand on either side, and standing in a golfer's stance, I asked him, "Sir, if I were to swing this bucket back to the right, abruptly, some of the water would spill out?" I demonstrated, making a little puddle in front of me. "Now, instead of starting so still, I will make a tiny move in the other direction, toward the target, creating the smallest of waves."

"When the wave hits the side of the bucket, I will start my backswing motion, following the wave back to the right. When I am all the way back, I will again follow the wave down and through." I demonstrated. It was an elegant, natural motion.

"Now you try."

It didn't take him long to get the general hang of it. At first the forward motion was too big, too dramatic. Once we toned that down he began to make the move perfectly, definite yet subtle.

I then asked him to try the move again but this time with his club. Again, at first it was overdone, with him pushing his hands too far forward. "You're close, that's the right idea." I told him. "This time I want you to make the forward press so you can feel it, but that I can barely see it."

I demonstrated a small rehearsal waggle. I wanted him to start to be aware of the center mass or weight of the club.

As I expected, his first waggles were overdone and stiff. "Sir," I said, "feel the weight on the end of the club, flowing back and forth like the water in the pail."

He began to make an elegant, almost artistic waggle.

As I watched, the term *proprioception* came to mind: *Awareness of one's body in space.* I was witnessing a student take learning to a level I had rarely seen before. It was stunning. His swing was evolving at a rapid pace.

He'd be ready for longer clubs by next week.

Review of golf session:

- 'Waggle' to feel the weight of the club.
- Instead of starting from a frozen position, you want to flow toward the target first, hands, body weight, whatever you choose. Make it subtle.

Naked at Taktsang

The spiritual history of Bhutan, from a Buddhist perspective, started in the 6th century, when *Padmasambhava* flew into the cave at Taktsang on a tiger, to subdue an evil being who was bugging the King. After turning the bad guy into a rock (a formation/mass now called Demon Rock), he figured that while he was here, he would also convert the King and all of Bhutan to Buddhism.

The monks who live there stay for three years but seldom leave. They live in the residential shelters, perched on the rock ledges. In the center are four main temples. The buildings are interconnected through rock stairways and steps, along with several wooden bridges.

Every morning at 4 am an old monk turns the prayer wheel, which is inscribed with holy chants. The sound of chimes accompanies the turning of the wheel.

In 1968, Chögyam Trungpa, the guru of my Rinpoche, wrote the famous *Sadhana of Mahamudra* there. The *Sadhana* is important because it brought together two traditions – one representing energy, another, space.

Rinpoche was the one who had suggested I visit the monastery, which I'd

Demon Rock.

heard was just 45 minutes to an hour up the mountain, on the cliffs surrounding the Paro Valley. It was a strenuous hike to say the least! It took me and my friend three hours. Meanwhile, young children and grandmothers alike passed us by with a cheerful "Good morning, sirs." One older woman even had two walking canes. She breezed by us like a sherpa.

Before we reached our destination, we passed a tiny house the size of a small kitchen, where the *Je Khempo*, the spiritual head of Bhutan, was born. We also passed a 300-yard-high waterfall and retreat huts for the monks, stuck into the rock face in ways that seemed to defy gravity.

Taktsang Monastery is a spectacular sight: Perched so precariously it seems glued onto the side of the mountain. It is made of wood that had to be carried up by hand or on a donkey's back. Some buildings were two storey and each one had a balcony with breathtaking views. It was like a fantasy.

When we arrived, a large group was just leaving and leading the way was a young teenaged boy who was totally naked; he wasn't even wearing shoes. I could only think that he was very poor.

Once inside, a monk took my group of four (myself, a journalist from California helping with the radio station, a nurse from Canada volunteering at the hospital and a DJ at the local radio station with the stage name Pink) through a series of shrine rooms. In the first, we followed Pink's lead and did three prostrations to the throne and three to the shrine. I made a note to ask my young teacher what I was bowing so deeply to.

The young Rinpoche had asked me to bring a photo – of Trungpa and another spiritual teacher, Khentse Rinpoche, standing together – and I now gave it to our guide. He looked at it for a long time, touched it on his forehead and immediately placed it in a prominent position on the shrine.

The second shrine had a statue representing long life, a bright red male icon sitting on a white lotus flower in full bloom, called *Amitayus*. I left a small donation of 70 ngultrum, or about one US dollar, again following Pink's lead. The next shrine was *Jambhala* representing wealth. This statue was about five feet high, made of solid gold, seated, with dark eyebrows and an incredibly ornate crown. He was surrounded by hundreds of small gold Buddhas. I left a bigger donation there, covering all the bases.

As my group was being shown around, I took the suggestion of my young student to go and meditate next to the upper shrine; what an incredible experience! I was on one of the balconies overlooking the 'heavenly realm of the *dakinis*', or angels; the mountains and the waterfall clear and pure as if the sky had melted. The amazing trees – white Himalayan birch, giant cypress as big around as a small putting green, the vultures, ravens, hawks, and eagles. A mountain, a perfect triangle, pierced the sky.

Once I got used to the view, my meditation was blissfully peaceful. Thoughts barely broke through to my consciousness but didn't stay. I was fully present, taking it all in, without any need for mental entertainment. Following my breath was enough.

After my session, which was only about 30 minutes, I rejoined my group and we decided to descend back to Pink's car, as we had been at Taktsang a couple of hours. We said goodbye to the monk who showed us around (in perfect English) and asked him why we hadn't seen the other monks. He told us they were on retreat, practicing intensely for a solid month. After my memorable short session, I felt a kinship with them.

On our journey back down the mountain, a young man passed us carrying on his back a load of wood about the size of a small car. When we reached the bottom, we took out a small picnic lunch. Then I saw the naked boy again,

Taktsang Monastery.

smiling and totally unashamed, When he walked by one group, they all began prostrating and lowering their eyes. Some put scarves around his neck, his only clothing.

Still naked, he got into a car driven by an older monk (who was fully clothed in robes) and as he was driven away, I asked someone who he was. I was told that he had no name but is a revered spiritual teacher who often comes to Taktsang Monastery. No clothes, no name. *Unattached* was the word that came to my mind.

Meditation session – cool boredom

At our next session, I told Rinpoche that I was lost in thought less often and had been able to stay with my breath one time for almost an entire meditation. "What struck me," I said, "was how boring it was!"

Rinpoche laughed for a long time. And when I asked if this was a typical experience for new meditators, he answered immediately and emphatically: "Yes! My teacher called it 'cool boredom.' He likened it to a mountain stream, cool and invigorating."

"The curious paradox is that when I accept myself just as I am, I can change."
—Carl Rogers

He continued: "In this era of the internet and constant entertainment, boredom is seen to be an awful state, to be avoided at all cost. This week when you practice, and when you notice your mind wanting to escape the simple act of following the breath, ask yourself what part of this present moment you are trying to escape. Dig a little deeper by sitting with the uncomfortable feeling of boredom. Just touch into it, then go back to the breath. Touch and go. Let us use the remaining time in sitting practice, using the touch and go technique."

As we sat, through my torrent of thoughts I was able to touch and then let go a few times. That seemed like progress.

The gong soon rang, signaling the end of the practice. Rinpoche then relayed a story.

"Ed, one of the great teachers of my lineage, Kyentse Rinpoche, was attending a Tibetan lama dance and being enthralled by the majesty of the performance. Right in the middle a man came up to him and started asking questions about meditation. Wanting to get back to the show, Kyentse gave the most direct answer possible: 'Look, when the past thought has ceased and before the future thought has started, there's a gap… PROLONG IT!'"

"Thanks for your efforts, until next time," my spiritual friend said softly.

We bowed, and I felt a wave of affection for this young man.

Review of meditation session:

- 'Cool boredom' is refreshing, not something to avoid.
- Prolong the gap between thoughts.

Sightseeing day – the strange beast

I was told that one of the 'must see' spots in Thimphu was the zoo, to see the *takin*, a four-legged grazing beast that is the national animal of Bhutan. According to my map, it wasn't too long of a walk from my apartment. So, one beautiful sunny Sunday, I packed some water and my camera and set off.

It wasn't long before I met up with a young Bhutanese fellow, splendidly dressed in a traditional gho, headed in the same direction. He greeted me with: "May I know you?" He introduced himself as Thinley and immediately took on the role of tour guide. He was a very cheerful, inquisitive teenager, headed into 9th grade. Thinley wanted to know about my family, did I have a car, do I like David Beckham or U2 and how big Maryland is.

We kept coming to forks in the road, and at every one he would say: "Takin up, sir." So we took the turns that went up, and up, and up. It wasn't long before my sea-level lungs were depleted, so we took a break and shared an orange. When I felt rested, he decided I needed the shortcut. "Takin up, sir," Thinley said, pointing at an extremely steep stairway that left the road and cut up through a little village. (In the dictionary, next to the word up, this stairway should be displayed!)

At the end of the vertical stairway we came to another road that was thankfully level. Here was Thinley's school, a traditional building beautifully

A takin.   Photo: Eric Kilby, Wikipedia

47

decorated with knots-of-eternity, the three jewels and other colorful iconography. Pointing down the road, Thinley said: "Takin down, sir."

"*Kaden che*," I replied, and went in search of the takin. It was a beautiful walk that took me by the estates of two cabinet ministers and a residence of the King. I saw families washing their clothes in a pristine mountain stream and then hanging them from the trees, while the children ran around playing.

I got to a fork in the road that was not marked, so I asked two young women strolling by which way to the takin. "Takin up, sir," they replied.

I hiked on for another half hour, the road continuing to climb. Stopping to rest, I watched a car continue up the road. Winding back and forth again and again, I realized that I had still a long way to go. The next time a taxi with an open seat passed by, I flagged it down. The ride to the top cost 50 ngultrum, or about one US dollar.

I hiked (up) around the perimeter of the fence that contained them, until I saw the oddest-looking creatures I'd ever witnessed, whose heads and bodies didn't seem to match.

The Motithang Takin Preserve is managed by the World Wildlife Foundation. It was originally a mini-zoo but turned into a preserve when it was discovered that the animals stayed there even when set free. It was set on a flat grassy area about the size of a football field surrounded by a strong link fence. In some areas of the enclosure were boulders that some of the animals were playing on. There was no charge to view the animals from outside the fence and there were fifty or so people looking in from all areas of the preserve.

According to legend, when the great saint Lama Druga Kinley, 'the divine madman', visited Bhutan in the 15th century, a large congregation of devotees gathered to witness his magical powers. The people urged the lama to perform a miracle. However, the saint, in his usual unorthodox and outrageous way, demanded that he first be served a whole cow and a goat for lunch. He devoured these with relish and left only bones. After letting out a large and satisfied burp, he took the goat's head, the only part he didn't eat, and stuck it onto the bones of the cow. And then with a snap of his fingers, he commanded the strange beast to rise and graze on the mountainside.

The takin were leaping like ballerinas from rock to rock. Occasionally one would roar – quite a funny sight with its mouth open and tongue sticking out. I found out the keepers call them 'goats with attitude'. I made the mistake, following the urging of some local Bhutanese men sitting on a bench, of placing my hand on the fence near one of these goat-antelopes. It charged the fence and banged it with his head, sending me backwards. The 'boys on the bench' roared with laughter.

This beast is so different that it is the only animal classified in its species, *budorcas taxicolor*. The 'Golden Fleece' from Greek mythology is from the takin.

Golf lesson – ball-flight laws

When I arrived at the monastery the next morning, Rinpoche was warming up. They were by far his best swings yet. When the bottom of the arc was too soon, he knew it and was able to get back to solid contact. The ball flight was lower, more penetrating. His swing had an elegant flow and was pleasing to watch. The miss was a hard pull, straight left. He was getting the clubface square, eliminating the need to flip the club at the ball.

"Rinpoche, it's time to get the driver out," I said, waving for the caddy to move further out, at around 150 yards. The first two swings were pop-ups, hit right off the roof of the driver. The third hit on the heel, starting straight then taking a U-turn to the right.

I didn't have my Flightscope radar machine, which I'd normally use to track the speed and spin of a ball, but I didn't need it. His club was swinging well left, with the angle of attack a good deal downward at impact. I would bet the spin rate was 6,000 revolutions per minute, two or three times higher than what is optimal.

Just like with thousands of students I taught before him, I needed to get Rinpoche's club coming more from the inside, with a level or even upward angle of attack. The first order of business was to explain to him the physical laws that make the ball do what it does – ball-flight laws.

I explained that the clubface is largely responsible for the starting direction of the ball, especially when using a driver.

"The ball will begin its journey 90 degrees to where the face is pointing, if you hit near the sweet spot," I told him. "Let's call that initial direction."

From there, the ball does one of three things: continue straight along that line, curve to the right, or curve to the left. If the path of the ball goes left of where the clubface is pointing, it will slice to the right. If the path goes to the right of where the face points, it will curve to the left.

In the previous three shots he'd taken, the ball started out going straight and then curved to the right. I asked him what that meant.

"It started straight at the target, so the face was straight. It curved to the right, so the path was to the left," he answered.

"Correct, well done," I told him. "From this point on everything we do with the driver will be dedicated to your learning to hook the ball, starting to the right of the target and hooking back in. So, what would impact have to look like to have that occur?"

"Face to the right of the target, path even more to the right of the face," he replied.

"Bingo!"

In order for him to practice this properly, I called on my stock drill. "Address the ball as before," I told him, "but this time move your feet until your back is facing the target. Your toes should be also pointing directly away from the target." I then drew a line in the sandy soil indicating an inside path for his club head to follow, and told him to make a swing that would feel like he would be sending the ball out to the right.

"OK, but shouldn't we move the caddy to the right?" he asked.

"Not necessarily," I answered. "Remember, the ball will start its journey where the face points."

His eyes lit up – he understood.

The first two swings were whiffs, not unusual for such an awkward stance. But on the third swing he did something he had never done before: he hit a hook that started a little right and curved back to the target. The ball sailed over Karma's head and rolled another 20 yards.

"You did it, Sir! Practice that for a week so your eyes get used to seeing a hook. We will begin to work on making that happen from a normal stance."

Review of golf lesson:

- Understand ball-flight laws.
- The clubface controls starting direction, the path-to-face relationship causes the ball to spin.
- A golf swing normally evolves from slice, to hook, then to straight.

English only ... and I'll try Dzongkha

It was the beginning of my fourth week teaching the juniors and I felt it was time to rev things up to the next gear.

Each group picked a name: Ravens, Takin, Snow Lions and Girl Power. It was the Ravens morning class; once they were assembled, I had them sit down on the grass, while I sat in a folding chair. "Does anybody know what the BYGA stands for?"

Most of them did, especially those who had been in the program for many years. "Correct, the Bhutan Youth Golf Association. And do you know that we are teaching you about some things that may be more important than golf? What do you think those are?"

Discipline came up, as did being respectful. Those are wonderful answers and in a sense correct, but not what I was looking for.

From the beginning, I didn't want to come in here assuming the role of North American savior, putting my code on an ancient civilization. But the world is changing quickly, here and everywhere else. In the new world, the smart will survive. (I was in the middle of reading Thomas Freidman's *The World is Flat*, which shows clearly that it no longer matters where you live if you want to take part in the global village).

"We are speaking English, which is the international language of commerce," I said. They could all get by in English and could understand me to a point. But as expected, when they spoke to one another, it was in Bhutanese.

"From now on, every Wednesday we will speak only English for the entire session. Love your language and speak it always. But for one-and-a-half hours a week, it will be English only."

"Yes, Coach," they replied. I could tell they thought this was a good idea and would give it a shot.

As the Wednesdays progressed, I could see them working harder and using their minds differently to get their points across. They took pride in being the one to teach me a new word, always trying to walk the fine line between too naughty and hilarious.

For example, *Che-you mindabu*, what you might say if someone fearlessly asks you for 50ng (about a dollar), has 'lost his forehead' (is not shy). Somehow this was slightly off color, always evoking a laugh if said by a *Chillup* (I was a *Chillup*, a come-from-away white person), and especially if you made the

Teaching the grip to the juniors.

gesture of putting your fingers together in the middle of your forehead, then almost throwing your forehead out into space.

These juniors worked hard and were extremely helpful. In their colorful phrasing I would hear: "I will help you that, sir," and "My team is winner-ing, Coach." A bogey was pronounced "boo-gey." A joke got the response "you tickle me." My all-time favorite, which I first heard spoken by my young guide to the zoo, was "May I know you?"

One student was curious about Christianity; it turns out he thought Mary was married to Santa!

Meditation session – finding my *self*

That week my meditation changed. I guess that's why they call it practice. I was getting better at noting, labeling and letting go.

My mind was less apt to hook onto a particularly attractive thought but rather let it rise and fall naturally.

Yet I still felt the boredom I had mentioned to Rinpoche and was unable to 'go deeper' as he had suggested. I blurted that all out on my next visit to the monastery.

Rinpoche got right to the point. "Ed, who is it that is bored?"

Oh boy, I thought, we are going off the grid now. I could sense we were entering new territory.

"Sir, I don't mean to be rude, but it is me, myself that is bored."

"What does your self look like?" he asked.

"Sir, that's obvious: You are looking at it." I tried not to sound frustrated as I was feeling that he might be playing games with me.

"Ed, if you lost an arm would it still be a self?"

"Yes, of course, Rinpoche."

"How about both arms and legs?"

"Heaven forbid, but yes, still me. But there goes my golf game!"

"Pare away everything else until nothing is left but your self. Tell me what it looks like."

I had never thought about me in those terms. The closest I could come up with was a tiny mini-me floating around someplace in my mind.

"Where in your mind?" he probed.

"Really, Sir, nowhere I can pin down. It's just there!"

I felt like he was taking me to a place where I was hanging onto my sanity by a thread.

"Let's sit together for 10 minutes," Rinpoche suggested. "See if you can find your self."

The session went quickly. I had practiced enough to be able to keep my mind in one place long enough to do the exercise he asked of me. When I did get distracted, I came back quickly to the search for my self, the little boss inside of me.

After he rang the gong, Rinpoche asked if I had found it.

> "No self, no self-con-sciousness."
> —Dr. Joseph Parent, PGA Tour coach and author of #1 best-seller *Zen Golf*

"Is it located anywhere?"

I had to answer no… it kept disappearing when I felt like I was getting close.

"Does it have a form, a place, a texture?" he asked.

Again I had to answer no. I couldn't find it.

"Ed, this was the practice of contemplation, not meditation. Your mind is tamed enough to look inward in that manner," he said, instructing me to end each of my meditations this week with five minutes of contemplation.

What am I getting myself into, and what is my self anyway? I thought. All I wanted was a better golf game! I didn't sleep much that night, searching for me. I had the feeling that how I now looked at the world was about to change, and that there was no turning back.

Review of meditation session:

- Look closely, is there a solid self somewhere inside of you?

Golf lesson – hitting the draw

I could tell Rinpoche had practiced. I just wondered when he found the time, as I was beginning to sense his schedule was jam-packed. (I learned from one of the few monks who spoke English that he might give many audiences every day, sometimes to students from North America and Europe. As well, he practiced meditation four hours a day).

His iron shots were again solid, but they pulled 40 yards to the left. The driver was hooking when he stood with his back to the target, but the slice returned when he assumed a normal stance.

That's where we would start. I explained how to do a modification of the hooking exercise we'd done before. "Now, Rinpoche, I want you to pull your right foot back a good 18 inches and turn your upper body at address so your chest points to the right of the ball, not the left of it like you used to. You are going to start with your back to the target."

Closing his shoulders in this manner would kick start the desired inside path.

Back home, I used training aids to teach players to come at the ball from the inside and promote a draw. Here, on this remote range, the only thing I could find was a rectangular, dried up piece of sod, about two feet long and a foot wide. I placed it on edge, a few inches outside the ball, slightly angled to the right.

I demonstrated that a swing that followed the correct arc could easily hit the ball on the sweet spot and miss the sod. But if it came from the outside, a collision of club with this piece of earth would occur.

I warned him to swing slowly as a) he would probably hit it and b) it could hurt. He must have taken 100 practice swings at varying speeds with his driver, clipping a tee with no ball on it. "Tee one up, Ed," he said, "I want to hit a real ball."

As I expected, he nearly whiffed the ball, knowing that his normal swing would have hit the sod. It hit right off the toe of the club, slivering off to the right.

He then took a few more slow motion swings, but this time drove it well over 225 yards, with a baby draw. He turned to me and smiled.

With all my high-tech equipment back home, an old dried up piece of sod did the job just as well. I could just imagine the ad on the Bhutanese Golf Channel: "For 3 payments of $19.95 you too can learn to hit a draw!"

Review of golf lesson:

- To come at the ball with a driver from the inside and hit a draw, set up with your back to the target. This is a drill that will change to a more normal stance over time.
- Training aids can be helpful in learning this.

Meditation session – *you* are not your thoughts

The next week when I went to the monastery, I was nervous. My meditation practice sessions had yielded nothing from my search for my self, and I wondered if I was failing.

"Sir, I was unable to find my self. Now what?" I asked when I sat down.

He chuckled at the way I phrased the question. "Now you are close to discovering what is under the boredom and perhaps why you get in your own way in the heat of battle on the course. Let's sit together for 10 minutes."

The meditation session went quickly, as I was becoming able to pay attention without distraction for longer and longer periods of time.

"Ed, where did your mind go in the times you were not with the breath?"

I thought for a second. "Well, I sing little musical ditties, mindless TV commercials, pop songs, whatever, in my mind," I admitted. "And they repeat over and over again. I go into the future, thinking how great I'm going to be after doing this work with you. I plan my future."

I continued, warmed up now. "And sometimes I go into the past, reliving embarrassing moments and recreating what I should have said or done."

"And then, occasionally, something shifts and everything opens up, and I feel like I am suddenly aware of everything at once. But it is not an overwhelming feeling, It's very pleasant."

"Well done," he said, catching me by surprise. With that long list of distractions, I really didn't think I was doing that great.

"This week I will ask you to begin to see the patterns: future, past, chatter in the present, loops you get stuck in, your detours," he said. "These different mental fixations might even evoke a reaction in your body; notice how that feels. In the short term, when you label a thought, add the type of thought, in your case: future, past, or distracted in the present. You are creating space between the thought and your reaction to it. If you believe the thoughts to be true

Body like a mountain

Breath like the wind

Mind like the sky

—Zen saying

56

and real, a storyline tends to develop. You're on the train, which takes you away to a whole story line."

"But as soon as you realize you are on the train," he said, "you have already stepped off."

We sat then for another 20 minutes, and I was able to notice how much I went into the future, with verses from Annie's 'Tomorrow' thrown in.

"Tomorrow, tomorrow, I'll love you, tomorrow …"

When he rang the gong and I got up to leave, Rinpoche was upbeat. "Be diligent, and jolly good work!" he said.

> ## Review of meditation session:
>
> • Not buying into thoughts creates space. Let them come and go without turning them into a story.

Golf session – body and arms in sync

Without the use of my usual high-tech teaching aides, I had to be inventive in how to get my point across. As a result, I could feel my instruction getting better, without relying on technology.

During our next lesson, I told him I wanted to work on getting his body and hands and arms to work in sync.

I took a swig from my 12 oz. plastic water bottle and held it out for him to see. "Here it is, the amazing two-in-one golf trainer," I said. "First, the body. Let me demonstrate."

I stood erect and placed the bottom of the half-empty bottle flat against my sternum, so it was horizontal to the ground. No water spilled out.

"If I bend over and stand properly at address, water will drain out," I said, making a small bending motion to demonstrate and glancing up to make sure he was following.

"However, when I turn back into my backswing, it will be close to level, and again no loss of water."

I demonstrated but stopped at the top of the backswing.

"Rinpoche, a good swing doesn't stop at this point; I just wanted to point out that even though the bottle is level, my shoulders are tilted a great deal, the right much higher than the left," I said. He nodded, getting it.

"Now, in the downswing, the water will spill, but quickly in the follow-through, no spill. In fact, at the very finish of the swing the bottle is pointed more upward."

I handed him a fresh water bottle and had him try it. Because his chest was in the right place, he easily fell back to his lead foot coming down in the transition from backswing to downswing. His finish was high and proud.

"Great!" I said. "Now, hands and arms."

To demonstrate the proper positioning of his hands and arms, I held the water bottle upside down in my right hand only, pointed like a club would be. Water started to drain out. I swung and folded my right arm and bent the wrist backward on itself. The bottle tilted slightly backward when my hands reached about rib cage high, but no water flowed out.

I did it again, filling the bottle up again, as most of the water was now gone. When my hand reached about hip high, the bottle titled back up and the flow stopped. In the downswing the water shot out on the ground where a ball would be. In the follow through, it stopped spilling.

"Your turn," I said.

I wasn't surprised when he did the move perfectly.

I then had Rinpoche hit some shots with an 8-iron, trying to duplicate the feel of that motion. They were the prettiest little knock-down shots you could ever imagine.

"It's a great drill, Ed, but there is a problem," Rinpoche said. "Bhutan is banning plastic bottles!"

Oh well, at least it was an honor to be in such an environmentally conscious nation. All agriculture in Bhutan is organic, and high-yield rice paddies are planted on mountainsides to save space, as well as to make them more water efficient (see page 65.)

Review of Golf Lesson:

- Train body and arm motion separately, then blend them together.

Meditation session – mixing mind with space

"Rinpoche, I was online looking up 'meditation' and I kept coming across the word mindfulness," I said at our next session. "Is what I am practicing called mindfulness?"

"Good question, and good timing," he replied. "The practicing you are doing is called *shamatha*, or mindfulness meditation. You are paying attention to the contents of your mind, non-judgmentally. You are watching how your mind, body and self works, without labeling anything as good or bad. Just noticing."

"In Buddhism, this is called 'taming the mind'. You could substitute the word bodyfull-ness for mindfulness."

"I think you are finding that this sense of paying attention is starting to infiltrate your daily life. You told me your wife notices, just in a Skype conversation. It is becoming a habit, a very good one. When you begin to enjoy it, it grows. Silence is delightful. Most of our thinking is a waste of time and energy, it gets us nowhere."

"Once you have somewhat tamed your mind to stay in one place for a period, something begins to naturally occur," he continued. "Remember when I asked you what was under the boredom? It's a sense of space, a bigger mind."

"Imagine trying to walk through a forest with roots and rocks everywhere, but you are carrying a glass of champagne. Mindfulness is taking care not to spill the contents, awareness is the big picture of walking without tripping. Awareness is more environmental, mind outside the individual ego."

"It is time to let some air into your practice, starting to work with the space," he then said.

He instructed me to shift my attention to the outbreath:

"When the breath goes out, follow it out, yourself, your mind, your attention. Let the breath, with you along with it, dissolve in the space. Mix your mind with space," he said.

"There is nothing either good or bad, but thinking makes it so."
—Shakespeare, in *Hamlet*

"All of man's difficulty comes from his inability to sit quietly in a room by himself."
—Pascal

"Stay out there until the next outbreath, then go out again. Out, dissolve, out, dissolve."

"Like before, if you get distracted by thoughts, label them then come back to the outbreath."

"This is called awareness – radiation without a radiator," he said. "Awareness is not yours, it is just there. It is a glimpse rather than a continuous state. If you hold onto awareness, it becomes self-consciousness."

He compared awareness to a candle lantern: "The flame is awareness and it is being protected from the wind by the glass of the lantern, which is the mindfulness," he said. "One needs the other. Mindfulness is not the whole story, but it is the starting point, and always the cornerstone."

During our meditation that session, I experienced an interesting occurrence: the sound of a yak mooing in the distance felt very close, as if it was originating within my body. After Rinpoche rang the gong I asked about this odd event.

"Ed, the great meditators of the past have discovered a truth difficult to grasp at first, that space and awareness are one. What you experienced was a direct experience of that. Your conscious, thinking mind will never comprehend what direct experience can know. It is called *drala*, and we will talk about this later once you have practiced at a deeper level."

"Jolly good work!"

And with that, we were done. I had to lot to think about. Walking home, I remembered a story told to me by Canadian coach Henry Brunton at a PGA dinner. He relayed a story of tennis great Ivan Lendl visiting his coach. The coach picked up a pencil, and handing it to Lendl, told him to study it during the upcoming week, reporting back with a full description.

A week later, Lendl came back with something like: "The pencil is yellow, octagonal, has an eraser attached with metal, the writing end is sharp and grey in color. The pencil

> "Be the breath, the breath is you."
> —Trungpa Rinpoche
>
> "Be the ball."
> —Ty Webb

says Eversharp on the side, in gold letters, and is 6 3/4 inches long."

"Fine," said his coach. "Now go back and look closer. Next week I want a 10 minute answer!"

Review of meditation session:

- Follow the outbreath, mixing mind with space.
- Mindfulness expands naturally to awareness.

Golf lesson – the trail leg is the governor

I had already decided that it was near time to get Rinpoche out on the course. But first, we needed to work a bit more on his form and had to clear the yaks off the range in order to be able to do it!

We started with some irons, working on getting the bottom of the arc in the right place. His left hand was holding the club too much in the palm and we adjusted it to just the base of the fingers, with 2 1/2 knuckles showing - the index, middle and sliver of the ring finger knuckles.

We then moved on to the driver, His set-up was good and he had a nice load back with some head rotation on his backswing (yes, one's head can rotate to help the turn).

But his right knee was losing structure, popping back away from the target. In addition, he was rolling his weight to the outside of his right foot. That meant there was no chance to fall back to the left. I explained that the backswing in golf was a lot like drawing a bow in archery; there is a stretch. If the hand and arm holding the bow buckle, the stretch would be lost.

I bent down behind him and placed my hand on his right knee, holding it in place as he swung back. I told him it was OK if the leg straightened some, as long as it didn't migrate to the right. I asked him to load his fully turned chest over that back knee and hit the ball.

Although I couldn't see the shot, the sound was unmistakable – he flushed it with a little draw.

"Sir, you are ready to go on the course. I'll see you at Royal Thimphu next week for a nine-hole round."

> **Review of golf lesson:**
>
> - The right leg is a governor of the swing. Where the right knee starts, it stays in the backswing, with only a little wiggle room.

Nine holes with the Generals

The Royal Bhutan Army is ever-present; they can be seen guarding government buildings and dignitaries. But unlike the military in other countries, these soldiers are also men and women of peace.

Many are devoted Buddhists. This military represents peace, not war. Yet they are highly trained – remember, Bhutan has never been invaded.

"The Dali Lama told me I would be reborn in a heavenly realm. At least I've got that going for me!" —Carl Spackler (a.k.a.) Bill Murray in the movie *Caddyshack*

"The army, which is trained by the Indian military, has only gone to battle once in the country's history, in 2003, in a conflict that lasted just days. While soldiers routed out rebel Indian militants camped along the border, news reports cited rituals and prayers for the Kingdom's safety going on throughout Thimpu."

—Rahul Bedi in New Delhi, *The Telegraph*

And these soldiers also love golf! On the Royal Bodyguard shooting range outside Dechencholing is a nine-hole course that could be the model for one of those calendars of fantasy golf courses. Cows mow the fairways, much as the sheep did at early St. Andrews in Scotland, the home of golf.

I kept hearing about The Generals, the three highest-ranking officers in the Royal Bhutan Army, who not only played golf, but also philosophized about this game that is such an enigma to many. A discussion over lunch with one of the Generals was about how golf mirrors life, with its good times and hard times, joys and disappointments. After lunch I was invited out for a game at their unique course.

This turned out to be one of the most memorable of the thousands of golf games I have played in my life. On some holes I felt as if I were looking at a fairway the width of a bowling alley, with a miniature green in the distance perched on a small mountain. In short – intimidating.

With a bag of clubs stitched together from the juniors' sets and the fact that I had been teaching golf more than playing it, it all showed in my performance. I played like a clown.

But it didn't seem to matter. The Generals were supportive, funny and super storytellers. It was a round of golf that felt like a great massage, or a wonderful meal. It flowed like honey.

I knew it was going to be a special day, when on the first hole, after topping a shot or two, I found my ball just short of the green. As I looked down at the ball I couldn't miss a large four-leaf clover, just behind my ball. All my life I have been looking for one of these, but until this moment had never found one. I picked it and carefully tucked it inside a small book to keep as a reminder of this special day.

Fittingly, on the last hole, Toli, the fifth member of our group (and who was not a General but a close attendant of the King), chipped in from a pretty impossible place (downhill lie, very little green to work with, in the rough, 10 yards away, over the green), to win the bets.

After the round, we walked to a meadow usually used for military training, where attendants served tea and rice. Perhaps someday that spot will become the officers' grill in the clubhouse.

Meditation session – self-consciousness

Sitting in the peaceful waiting area outside of Rinpoche's quarters, a realization hit me like a bolt of lightning: This young Buddhist holy man was my friend. I felt a wave of love and devotion for him that surprised me and I wondered if this was what people meant when they talked about having a guru.

Rinpoche's attendant, Tashi, soon escorted me in, and as usual, I sat down across from him. With an elegant wave of his hand, he signaled for me to begin the conversation.

"Sir," I began, "as I sat this week my normal mind activities occurred. A few minutes in I had reached the boredom level with not much going on. But

"Boredom is part of the discipline of meditation practice. This type of boredom is cool boredom, refreshing boredom. Boredom is necessary and you have to work with it. It is constantly very sane and solid, and very boring at the same time. But it's refreshing boredom. The discipline then becomes part of one's daily expression of life. Such boredom seems to be absolutely necessary. Cool boredom."
—Trungpa Rinpoche

this time, rather than avoiding it, I allowed the boredom to exist with space, as you showed me."

At first, I told him, it was just conceptual; I was mimicking the idea of surrounding my mental state with space. But then something shifted: "Suddenly I was able to stand apart from wanting it to be different and just let it be," I said.

The bored feeling melted away, exposing a more basic mind state.

I described it like a 'big layer of something sticky, like flypaper' at the bottom of my mind. "It had the feeling of a giant level of self, the all-pervasive me all spread out and coloring everything that happened above. The sticky quality was my desire to hold on to what passed through my mind," I said.

When I stuck with this image, I told him, it shifted. "It turned out to be me watching me," I said. The flypaper changed into a film or a giant eyeball that constantly monitors my every move and thought, criticizing, commenting and judging.

"I found the layer below boredom," I said, "and it was not pleasant."

"But I now know that I found the cause of my yips: I was watching myself so closely on the course that I was too self-conscious. I could not breathe."

I stopped then, a bit worked up.

"Jolly good," was Rinpoche's only response.

I had not expected such a lighthearted answer and felt a bit put off that he did not take my discovery more seriously. But once I realized that my reaction was, well, reactionary, I appreciated how his easy acceptance of my experience also lightened the mood.

He then moved on. "We hold our subconscious in our body," he said. "In your daily activities, pay attention to your spine being upright, your front being soft. Notice when you feel like bending over and hiding."

Rice paddies.   Photo: Haiyan Dai, Instagram haiyan0819

I nodded. I also had a question I'd wanted to ask him if we had time. During my Google research, I discovered that he was renowned for teaching something called *Dream Yoga*. "Can you tell me what that is?" I asked him.

He said it is a practice of being able to direct one's dreams rather than un-consciously being buffeted around. It was formally introduced by Naropa, a great Tibetan teacher from his lineage in the 11th century and then written about by an Indian teacher named Lawapa ('Master of the blanket').

"Most practitioners use it as a time to deepen their meditation practice, but you could explore anything you like in that practice," he said. "I have been working on my golf game at night for a while now!"

He told me that when my own meditation practice was stronger, he'd tell me how to do it. "For now," he said, "see if you can remember your dreams. Keep a pad of paper and pencil by your bedside and write them down first thing upon waking up."

I had studied the work of Austrian psychologist Karl Jung, who believed dreams were a direct path to self-actualization, so I was intrigued by this potentially new practice.

And I now had a glimpse into how my young student was improving at such an astonishing pace.

Review of meditation session:

• Self-consciousness occurs when we believe our thoughts about ourselves to be true, and we beat ourselves up for not matching up to our ideas of how we should be.

MONTH TWO

Golf lesson on the Royal Thimpu Golf Course

It was January in Thimphu, and the weather was beautiful. Being in the mountains, I expected the temperature to be cooler, but the latitude offset the altitude.

Our work moving forward had to be on how to score: different lies, shots around the green, course management. As far as the mental game, that important 'inner game', I had more to learn from Rinpoche than he did from me. But when it came to swing work, he still needed some attention.

The Royal Thimpu Golf Club is a fun layout and very playable. It was designed by Ron Freem, an American designer from California, who has done some fine courses all around the world. It is a nine-hole gem.

Rinpoche arrived wearing his robes, as he did during our meditation sessions – not your typical attire for golf. Luckily, Royal Thimpu's dress code had no exclusions, as many of the golfers wore the traditional robe-like gho.

I am not a fan of playing lessons; unless the golfer can hit the ball with some degree of consistency, what's the point? On a busy course we can't really stop and work on fixing a slice. But I wanted to see how far Rinpoche had progressed so that I knew what to work on with him.

The first hole is a downhill 130-yard par 3. We discussed how to assess a hole, consider where the trouble is, i.e. water and other places you don't want to go, pin position and the notion of green light, yellow light and red light. In other words, when to play safe and when to be aggressive. I hit first and my pitching wedge sailed right over the pin to the back of the green. It usually took me a few shots to remember that the ball carried much further in this altitude; we were at 7,000 feet after all!

Rinpoche was not sure whether to use a 7 or 8-iron. I suggested he take the 7 and tee the ball two club lengths back from the front of the tee box, making his opening tee shot a few yards longer. Why not show him how, knowing the rules can help him?

The ball was well struck but pulled a little, so his ball missed the green pin-high but still in chipping range.

One of the reasons I like to teach the short game on the course is because there are so many options. "You have lots of choices here," I told him. "The fringe is cut short, so you could putt. But the grain is against you, so the ball might get caught up and finish short of the hole. You could hit a high pitch, but the landing area is narrow and into a bank. There is a lot of green to work with and only a few feet to carry to the green."

"Sir, take out your hybrid." The advent of the hybrid, a shorter club with more mass in the head, not only helped golfers with the long approach shots but also gave more options around the green. He reached for the 6-hybrid and I instructed him to hold it like a putter and hit it like a putt.

His stroke was beautiful and he hit the ball solidly. The movement of his legs was excessive but not a deal breaker. The ball skimmed over the fringe to the putting surface, rolling up a few feet to the left of the pin.

My putt was downhill, with very little break. The ball rolled up a few feet away from his. But when I went to finish the shot, that old, dark feeling came over me. I was getting the yips and there wasn't even any pressure on me!

Maybe I wanted to shoot a good score to show him how my mindfulness practice was paying off. (Clearly, it wasn't.)

I took my address and just like that Open qualifying day in Washington, I couldn't draw the putter back. Somehow, even though my hands twitched, I managed to knock it into the hole, hoping Rinpoche didn't notice my angst.

He then popped his ball right in the middle of the hole.

The second hole is a fine par 4, possibly the hardest on the Royal Thimpu course. My swing was feeling good. I smoked a drive down the right side – it finished in the rough but with a good angle to the pin. Rinpoche again teed off in the middle of the markers. His pre-shot routine was taking way too long and I decided to talk to him about that at a later lesson. He hit a solid drive but it pull-hooked, ending up in some bushes on the left.

Since we had the course to ourselves, I decided this was a good time to stop and discuss course management, and specifically, where to tee up to maximize the landing area on a drive.

"Sir, teeing in the middle is not always the ideal spot," I said. "If you are hitting a hook, going to the extreme left side of the teeing ground gives you a much better angle and opens up the fairway. Likewise, if you slice, the right side would offer a better angle." I had him hit another from the right side of the tee; that one finished in the middle of the fairway.

When we got to his first drive, it was sitting in a tangle of wild cannabis bushes, but the sharp-eyed caddy found it. It was unplayable.

I described his options for an unplayable lie: Drop straight back away from the hole, drop two club lengths away, no closer to the hole, or go back to the tee - all with a one stroke penalty. He chose to drop two club lengths away, no closer to the hole. He stepped up to hit a 3-fairway metal when I stopped him, thinking the time was right to discuss club selection.

"Rinpoche, you hardly checked at the situation your ball is in," I began. "Look closely: It is in a slight indentation with heavy grass around it. You could hit that 3-metal 100 times and 100 times it would be a miss-hit. In this situation you need a club with some loft, just to get it out to the fairway."

He chose the 8-iron and hit it as well as can be expected from that lie. The ball was advanced about 90 yards, leaving a short iron in.

My approach was pin-high on the green, about 20 feet to the right. Hitting greens was not my problem.

He had a straightforward chip with lots of green to work with, but skulled his wedge, the ball rolling over the green.

"Sir, my suggestion is to take out your pitching wedge and play it in near your back foot with a very narrow stance. Lean the grip end of the club slightly forward so it is adjacent to your left thigh. Lift your hands higher than normal, so that the heel of the club is slightly off the ground," I said,

"Steering, ie like a steering wheel, precludes and leads to the yips."
—PGA Tour Coach David Orr

demonstrating with my own club as he moved his hands into position. "Now it's like a putt – a shallow stroke with a long flat spot."

I was teaching him the low-spin chip that the short game wizard Paul Runyan taught me.

He hit it perfectly, leaving a 5-foot uphill putt.

I felt like I had a good read on my next shot: right to left – away from the spectacular mountains – what I call a 'speed putt.' I got a little greedy and ran it three feet by.

Rinpoche next banged his 5-footer right in the center of the hole. I was jealous of his fearlessness.

Standing over my little putt, I knew I had no chance. I tried to calm down and be with my breath, but my hands were shaking. In weeks of meditation practice, this mental state never arose. The best I can describe it was that I felt afraid, as if expecting impending doom.

My ball never came close to hitting the hole.

I turned and looked at my teacher. "Sir, this is exactly what happened to me that day many years ago. This is why I quit tournament golf."

He looked genuinely concerned. "What's the image that comes to mind when this happens, what does that feeling look like?"

What first came to mind was of a person being bullied, but I'm the bully. And fear creeps up my body until I can't move. I'm frozen with fear. I told him all of this.

"It's just you and me, no tournament on the line. The scores won't be in the papers tomorrow," he said gently. "Look at that state of mind as you would on the cushion. Don't try to change it, or ignore it, simply let it be. Above all, don't try to fix it. When we meet again for meditation instruction, we will be doing an ancient practice called Demon Work. For now, your job is to get to know that feeling intimately."

I wasn't sure I liked the sound of 'Demon Work,' but I had to admit I felt relief at being able to describe what happens to me. I saw a sliver of hope that this was a step in the right direction.

Review of golf lesson:

- Assess the lie on fairway shots.
- Tee on the side of the tee box that gives you the best margin for error. Two club lengths back is an option when between clubs.

Meditation session – dealing with feelings

After a ten minute sitting practice, Rinpoche began to speak.

"The main practice to start is simply paying attention to the breath and coming back each time you leave. If you lose your mind, just come back," he said. "Only when you can tame your mind, can other practices be done effectively."

"Feelings are at the root of the practice; meaning, identifying them when they arise," he continued. "If you get swept up in a feeling, it leads to thoughts which lead you away from this moment."

"To get rid of your feelings, feel them."
—Sigmund Freud

"Feelings are hardwired in us, they are our birthright," he said. "They can be beautiful, adding color to human life. But they can also lead us down some destructive paths."

"Meditation is a way to allow us to experience feelings, without being hijacked by them," he explained.

"Feelings are seductive, they're juicy. But just like thoughts, feelings arise and naturally fall away – unless you hold onto them. Touch them, acknowledge them, then come back."

I took that in but was curious about something else.

"Sir, what about negative thoughts?" I asked. "I can't get rid of them."

"Negative thoughts are no different than any other thought," Rinpoche said. "We are human, and parts of our brain are still trying to protect us from dangers that aren't there. The problems arise when you believe negative thoughts are bad."

Monks at Cheri Monastery.

I had to admit that I did and told him so. He nodded.

"Have you ever had a negative thought on the course and still hit a good shot?"

"All the time," I answered.

"The negative thought cannot affect you," he said, "unless you overlay on top of it the thought that it is bad. Just notice and go back to feeling your body."

He invited me to sit again and told me that when a thought arises, to see if I can discover the feeling associated with it. "Experienced meditators see a feeling arise and fall before a thought happens," he said. "When you get to that level," he added, "thoughts will not lead you around by the nose."

He rang the gong again and I began the process of breathing. And when a thought dragged me away from the breath, I tried noticing that I had left, labeled it thinking, and then came back. As I sat, I started becoming more aware of the feelings under the thoughts than of the content of the thoughts themselves.

My thoughts about the future seemed to have a feeling of

Trungpa Rinpoche, was asked on a TV program, "What is meditation?"

His answer: "Meditation is noticing the space between you and the TV screen."

impatience, which seemed to come from trying to escape boredom. Negative thoughts, things in my life that weren't just right, came out of a feeling of fear.

The songs in my head also seemed to come from boredom, filling up the space with theme songs of TV sitcoms.

Review of meditation session:

- Feelings are powerful but are still to be considered thoughts. Feel them, then come back to the breath. Touch and go.

Golf lesson – pitching is a pivot

For our next golf session we met back at the monastery field. I poked a stick in the ground 40 yards out and emptied the ball bucket onto the ground.

"Rinpoche, I want you to understand those less-than-full shots. Try to land the ball on the stick."

As he had done on the course, he pretty much made every mistake there is: on one shot he hit the ground so early and hard he only moved the ball 10 feet, the next was a shank right off the heel of the wedge. The next shot he grazed the top of the ball, rolling it past the stick. When he finally hit one on the club face, the ball flew 20 yards too far past the stick.

His mistakes were typical. He swung the club too vertically in the down-swing and too far back. His body stalled through the ball, no pivot whatsoever which meant he had to straighten his right arm too soon to catch up.

I explained that by going too far on the backswing, you then have to de-celerate your body turn when you reach the ball. And this shot calls for a very active body, especially through impact.

I held up a club adjacent to his right shoulder and asked him to do his backswing again. Going back too far, his left arm would whack into the club.

"It's surprising how what I feel I am doing is not what I am actually doing," he said. I nodded. I first heard Butch Harmon say 'feel and real are different', back in the '90s.

The second task was to get his shaft less vertical. When a swing is shorter the club shaft has got to be angled back on the correct pitch, as there is no time for corrections. If his swing was a house, he was swinging on the wall, when he needed to swing on the roof, less vertical.

"Take it back with your left arm only, just to 9 on a clock," I explained. "Now, Sir, feel the weight of the club wanting to pull itself down back away from the ball and less vertical. Don't fight it – if your arms are relaxed it will naturally happen."

He did it, and the club pointed 45 degrees at the ball. "Hit a few one-handed," I suggested.

He hit the ball so well that we joked maybe he should play his wedges that way. "Now keep that feeling but with two hands," I instructed.

He got the club angle right but was not opening his body enough through impact.

I learned the pitch shot from my mentor in Maryland, Bill Strausbaugh. He called it 'controlled pull away'. I shared this with Rinpoche. "Think of your left arm and the club handle. At impact you want the end of the lever, or your left shoulder, as far away from the ball as it can be, thereby pulling straight back on the handle. Don't worry, you won't top or miss it."

I had seen a lot of monkeys in the mountains around Thimphu. I told him, "If one of those monkeys were to drop on your left shoulder as you were hitting a pitch, imagine how vigorously you'd fling that guy up in the air and backward just by turning your chest."

It took him nine or ten shots to feel the timing of the monkey toss. Once he did, though, he started throwing darts at the stick, nearly hitting it every time.

I asked him where he felt the action. "I feel pressure between my left pec and the inside of my left arm," he said.

"You got it, Sir!" I cheered.

I told him to practice from 40, 50 and then 60 yards, with a goal of Karma not having to walk too far to pick up balls. "If you hit it fat, or ground the club too early, chances are you straightened your right arm too soon," I reminded him. "So when you get the 'fats' think about keeping your right arm bent until the ball is struck. Later we will work on the shorter, finesse wedges."

Review of golf lesson:

- The distance wedges are pivot-based. Go shorter on the backswing and turn through, keeping a feeling of pressure under the left armpit.

Meditation session – basic goodness

"Any questions, Pro?" Rinpoche asked after our meditation.

I did have some. I told him that during the week, I'd experienced some strong emotions during my practice sessions. "As much as I tried to change, to get back to the breath, the emotions stayed. Do you have any suggestions?"

I had the brief thought that he had probably heard that question hundreds of times before.

"Ed, if you were to look closely, there is some subtle resistance to the emotions you wish would go away," he began. "There's the pain of the emotion, which is straight-forward and real. Then there's the pain you put on top of that, which is not wanting or not accepting the emotion."

"If you leave the emotion alone and don't push it away," he said, "you will start enjoying your mind."

He explained that the original pain can be dealt with directly by just noticing it without judging it as good or bad, or by trying to escape it.

"Ed," he said then, "you clearly set out my path to better golf: first making contact, then fixing the slice, then fixing the hook, then distance control. I am only in the middle of that process, but I feel a quality of being on a journey."

"Similarly, the practices I am showing you are also a journey. You are in the taming-the-mind phase and frankly, that will always be the basis of any movement forward."

"Next will be training the mind, which we are beginning to get into. That is the space, the expansion. The word for that in Sanskrit is *vipassana*."

"Ed, when you came here, you wanted to understand why you froze under pressure. That's all. I think you are seeing that there's more to the mind."

I had had the same thought earlier in the week. I even had a meditation session where I did not think about golf even once.

"Suddenly, almost unexpectedly, a wider space opens up."

"There is a feeling of something being born in us, expanding and waking up. That experience is the birth of bodicitta."
—Osel Tendzin,
Buddha in the Palm of your Hand

"In Buddhism we talk about the view, or the underlying reason you do something," he continued. "I would like to offer you a view to start with. The view is personal so this might change as your practice deepens."

"I suggest you take the attitude toward your thoughts that they are visitors, while the gap, that moment you come back to the breath, is your home. As they pass by, acknowledge the thoughts, say hi and be friendly and just let them go. Don't invite them in for dinner and conversation."

"Be curious as they come and go," he said. "They are not the enemy and they'll always come around. Touch and go; touch the thought then let go."

"Like a fawn you happen upon in the woods, notice it flicking its ears and watch it without scaring it away. It will leave on its own," he said.

He explained that I was beginning to uncover layers in my mind, like peeling an onion. I got down to boredom and found that if I stayed with it long enough it changed into a vague, general sense of self.

"There is one more layer that you will soon discover," he said. "That layer is your birthright, your essence. It is called basic goodness and it connects you with the entire universe."

"Take away all your accomplishments, failures, history, future plans," he said, "Strip it all away and what is left is a human being, standing on the earth, breathing. You are worthy of being here."

He was quiet for a minute, then said, "Let us sit for 10 minutes."

Usually I was so in my own head during practice that I didn't notice anything outside of my mental chatter box. But today for whatever reason, I was very aware of Rinpoche. He was sitting like a mountain, unmoving, solid. I could feel his depth and it brought me down in a good way, from being up in my head to somewhere deeper, calmer, and it felt wonderful.

When Rinpoche rang the gong, I remained in that incredible space for a moment longer, then blurted out, "I think I did it Sir, I think I finally understand what meditation is about, what you have been telling me!"

He looked at me kindly, like a grandfather might look at a five-year-old. It wasn't one bit condescending but had the flavor of an important teaching about to arrive.

"Ed, you have practiced long enough now to have had glimpses that thoughts and experiences are temporary. The most painful state of mind passes ... as does the most blissful."

"Always come back to the view. Say hello to the thought, give it a smile, but don't invite it in. Go back to the breath, to your home of basic goodness, that place where all thoughts are equal."

Review of meditation session:

- You are not your thoughts. There is something deeper.
- Underneath all the layers—your thoughts, feelings, identity—there is something deeper. There's a basic goodness.

Chortens on the course

On the Thimphu course are three chortens. A chorten, sometimes called stupa, was described to me as a spiritual monument of sorts, a representation of an 'awakened mind'.

These three chortens are well over 600 years old and still in surprisingly good condition. They are kept up and painted regularly. The biggest is on the 6th hole, a very nice par four, dogleg to the left.

The problem for golfers is its placement relative to the hole. A good drive, but slightly pulled, will smack right into it. On the first playing round with the juniors, one student, Tashi, did just that. Had the chorten not been there, the shot would have beautifully cut the corner, shortening the hole considerably. Instead, his ball rocketed backward and into a lake. It was a double penalty for Tashi: a lost ball and stroke-and-distance.

"The visual impact of the stupa on the observer brings a direct experience of inherent wakefulness and dignity. Stupas continue to be built because of their ability to liberate one simply upon seeing their structure."
—Chögyam Trungpa Rinpoche

Teaching the juniors, a field trip to "Dog Mother's" clinic

My work with the juniors was becoming more rewarding, as many of them started to develop into better golfers. Attendance at the clinics was growing, as word of mouth was attracting more students.

I had been hearing for months now from the kids about the 'Dog Mother', or in Dzongkha, *Rochi Ama*. Born in France, her name was Marianne Guillet. She ran a clinic that took in animals in need. It turns out she was an architect and a geographer, with some medical training, but for humans, not animals. She has treated over 30,000 animals; monkeys, cows, deer, pigs, horses and cows. But the majority of her work was with dogs.

In Bhutan, dogs are everywhere, cared for by everybody, but not always by one owner. In the evenings it was sometimes hard to sleep, as they howled at the moon in unison. Many were underfed and unhealthy. So 'Dog Mother' took them in.

I contacted her about taking the juniors to her clinic, the Pilou Medical Center, for one of our monthly field trips.

The juniors and I piled into a bus and an hour later arrived at the foot of a mountain. As we hiked up the trail to the clinic, dogs started to follow us, first only a few, but by the time we reached the top, there were easily 50 dogs surrounding our group of 20 children.

And these dogs were not wagging their tails, happy to see us. With fangs bared and growling, the dogs made me fear for our safety. They were protecting their turf from invaders and it was downright scary.

Finally, in a quiet voice, I asked the kids to slowly turn around and head back down and they seemed happy to oblige. Rochi Ama is doing compassionate work for thousands of animals in need, and in turn, they are the security guards for their 'Mother'.

Golf lesson – putting on the brakes for distance control

For my next golf lesson with Rinpoche, we were again back at the monastery. The range was in great condition – the yaks must have been hungry.

"Rinpoche, I would like for you to play leapfrog," I instructed. "Hit the first shot 20 yards with your sand wedge. Hit the next shot to land just beyond the first. Continue that process to about 50 yards."

His technique was looking much better and the contact acceptable. But his distance control was still lacking. His swing didn't seem to have much punch at impact. The best wedge players strike the ball with authority, even on less than full shots.

"Sir, as we discussed last week, it is a swing with a strong turn through the ball, not so much a sweep," I said. "I want you to try the same drill but cut short the finish."

The fact is: The work is done by the time the club is level to the ground in the through-swing.

I suggested he use the mantra 'when the turn stops, the arms stop'. Stopping abruptly like that is a great way to control the distance while still making a dynamic strike. This is also a way to learn to put on the brakes. Creating club speed has two components: acceleration as well as rapid deceleration.

He tried the leapfrog game again, with much better results. "Ed, you have just dispelled another tip given to me by well-meaning friends: Always swing to a full follow through."

"The accelerate-decelerate feeling will not only help your pitching, it is also a path to hitting the ball farther," I replied. "See you tomorrow, Sir."

Review of golf lesson:

- On distance wedge shots, stop the arms when the turn stops.

Meditation session – walking meditation

"Today we will start with a 10-minute meditation, then I would like to introduce what's called meditation in action," Rinpoche told me when I sat down.

When I started working with him two months ago, I was fidgeting after only a minute or two of practice. Today when he rang the gong, I felt like his timing was off.

"Was that really 10 minutes?" I asked him. "It passed incredibly quickly."

He smiled. "That is not unusual. Time changes. You could say that at a certain level, it becomes subjective."

I didn't know if I could get my head around that notion. Isn't time always constant – a second is always a second? Was he telling me that I can change reality? I stored that question for a later date.

Rinpoche then stood up and gestured for me to do the same.

"When we did sitting practice, the first step was to feel the pressure points: bum on cushion, hands on thighs," he said. "I want you to do the same here. Feel your feet on the ground and the sense of balance. Let your balance settle."

After a few moments, he said we were to walk slowly around the shrine hall. "Instead of the breath," he said, "you are feeling the motion of striding: the heel, then toe pushing into the ground and then a stride with the other leg and again the pressure of heel, then toe touching earth.

"If your mind wanders, as it always will, gently notice and bring it back to the stride. Even though we are walking slowly, a definite rhythm will emerge: Stride, heel, toe, movement, stride, heel, toe."

"Now walk with me for 10 minutes."

My mind started racing. Wow, I can do this during a round, meditating the whole way. I am going to be unstoppable. I was entering old thought patterns, a place my mind goes for entertainment.

Caught up in that reverie, I started walking faster and faster without realizing it. Before I knew it I had caught up to Rinpoche, who was walking in front of me, and had to slow my pace or else step on his robes.

I realized at that moment my mind had temporarily 'left the building'.

After our next lap around the room, Rinpoche settled back onto his cushion and rang the gong. I went back to my seat.

"Ed, add this practice at the end of your 30-minute sitting practice. Do three or four circles around your practice room. But try not to break the speed limit!" He paused and I knew that I had been busted.

"This is a very powerful practice," he continued. "Do not think of it as lesser than regular sitting. It is a way that you will be able to bring your training into your daily life, golf included."

"Wherever we walk, we can practice meditation. This means that we know that we are walking. We walk just for walking. We walk with freedom and solidity, no longer in a hurry. We are present with each step. And when we wish to talk we stop our movement and give our full attention to the other person, to our words and to listening."
—Plumb Village Mindfulness Practice Center

"It is better to travel well than to arrive."
—Gautama Buddha

> **Summary of meditation session:**
> - Walking meditation is not just exercise or a break from real meditation. It *is* real meditation.

Golf lesson – slow motion learning

In all my years of teaching, I had never had a more adept student. Rinpoche was able to control his body at a level even I could not do. For example, one of my go-to drills when making a change in a golfer's habitual pattern, is slow-motion swings. Most people's idea of slow motion is just a little slower than normal. The first time Rinpoche did this exercise, his swing took two minutes!

What the drill brings up are those 'black out' areas in your swing, where you really don't know what is happening with your body. And for Rinpoche, it was the transition.

His backswing was fine, deep and fully loaded, the face of the club square at the top. But coming down his hands and the club still got a little outside and away from his body. He was able to come from the inside through sheer will-power, but it was a contrived, forced swing. It caused him to go, as Strausbaugh would say, 'belly up', or in current teaching vernacular, into early extension of the hips.

I asked him if there were any points in his swing that he was unclear on, after the slow swing exercise. He answered: "Yes, that point where the backswing ends and the down-swing begins."

"Sir, a couple of things must occur in this critical spot," I began. "Your arms should be still moving back as you put pressure into the ground under your lead foot. It is such a fine timing that even the best players get off-sync from time to time."

"I understand that Buddhists do not kill even bugs, but where I teach back home, I tell people to 'squish a bug' with their left foot to begin the downswing. You could insert

There is nothing inherently wrong with coming out of your spine angle, or "belly up." After all, the man who won the most majors ever, Jack Nicklaus, did it. So did Payne Stewart.

It's a function of the amount of hip turn through impact.
—the author

'squish a soft drink can'," I added.

"Immediately after that you will begin to feel the same feeling you had in pitching: pressing the left arm against the chest as the chest turns through. If your shoulders are tilted to the right degree, this motion will bring your arms to the ball perfectly. For today if you can get that feeling of pushing into the ground with your left foot, that would be a wonderful start."

I had him hit a few shots with my favorite drill: swing back, lift the left foot completely off the ground and immediately plant it back down, like an elephant stepping, heavy and solid. Planting it down even before the left arm goes parallel to the ground in the backswing.

I left him with instruction to practice the drill throughout the week and told him that next week we'd build from there.

Review of golf lesson:

- A slow-motion swing, done mindfully, can reveal your blind spots.
- The transition begins by putting pressure early into the lead foot.

Meditation session – consistent schedule

Waiting in the anteroom had become a practice in itself. I knew I would be on the spot, so to speak, so my mindfulness was intensified. It had the feeling of the warm-up before the last round of a big tournament.

Tashi invited me in and as I took my customary seat, my teacher opened with, as usual: "Tell me about your practice, Ed."

I realized that my questions were becoming subtler. I had the vague thought that this seemed to match my awareness of my mind becoming more subtle. I told him that my week had been so busy, that I had missed two days of meditation. "Do you have some advice for when busyness gets in the way of practice?"

He chuckled. "My North American students ask this question a lot," he said. "My answer is that your intention is most important. Every day at least set foot into the room where you do your daily practice. And either practice as normal or state out loud why you will be unable to practice that day. Even if you only have time for ten, five, or even one minute, that would be good.

"There comes a time when you will realize how important this is on your list of daily priorities, and in fact the to-do list of your day will be better served when your mind is tamed."

I took that in. "I had a session last week where my thoughts and emotions were intriguing me," I told him. "Rather than being carried away, I was curious, following the patterns instead of the content. I felt very refreshed after the session and that curiosity continued through the day. It was really cool!"

"Jolly good. Any other questions?"

"Yes, one more. I believe I am an unlucky golfer. Putts lip out way more than my fare share and I never seem to get the breaks. I have a friend, Bucky, who is the opposite – the luckiest player I've ever seen. We call it 'The luck of the Buck.' How can I get luckier?"

He thought a while. It almost seemed like he was going into deep meditation judging by the energy that seemed to build around him, which was palpable.

"My teacher, Trungpa Rinpoche, spoke of the term *drala*. When you walk in the woods and hear the wind in the trees, sometimes natural sights, sounds and feelings can stop your mind with their power. That is drala: pure perception."

I heard him say: "Letting go is relaxation based on being in tune with the environment, the world. Fire is hot. Water is wet. Wind is flowing. Earth is solid. Truth exists at that level."

"It could be a rock, a river, or the ground under your feet. Suddenly you find you are intimately connected to the natural world, not separate. It could be called blessings – blissful and beautiful."

"Just like luck, you can't crank up drala, but it is everywhere. If you are open and ready, the dralas will rain down, magic waiting to happen."

"Let's call it 'luck' for a moment. It's waiting to happen, but if you are not ready, it will find another player. Be patient, drala is looking for you. Just continue to do your

> "Letting go is relaxation based on being in tune with the environment, the world."
> —Trungpa Rinpoche

job, continue to show up for your piece of it. And when the dralas show up, be ready."

> ### Review of meditation session:
>
> - A consistent place and time for your practice is recommended.
> - If you can't practice that day, at least peek your head into the room and say why. Even one minute of practice would be helpful.
> - Drala is everywhere. Be open and it will find you.

Golf lesson – frisbee toss

"Let's go back to the frisbee throw," I said when I saw Rinpoche next. I handed him the pie tin. "Now wind up as if you were going to throw it a mile left-handed, but don't throw it."

He did so, and as he neared the full wind up, he pushed back onto his left foot, putting pressure there.

"Sir, did you see how nearly impossible it is to just turn back and stop?" I asked him. "You naturally moved back into the left side. You didn't unwind, but there was an unmistakable shift back."

I asked him to pick up his golf club, turn back as if he were throwing the frisbee and feel the pressure go down into his left foot early in the transition. Then I had him do this over and over until he got the feeling. This subtle movement of the pressure going left into the ground is what separates good ball strikers from poor ones. It's not really a big shift of body mass, but rather putting pressure into the ground under the lead foot, early.

The difficulty in learning a quick motion like a golf swing is noticing subtle thoughts while performing this complex motion. It helped that Rinpoche's meditation practice made him proficient in noticing everything that goes on in his body and mind.

I asked Rinpoche to again hold the frisbee in his left hand and to notice what happens after the pressure went left into the ground.

"Ed, as soon as I feel the pressure in the ground, I have the urge to unwind my chest," he said. "I am feeling it between my left shoulder and left hip. I also feel my hips wanting to unwind and what I can only describe as a snap, while I simultaneously feel like I'm pushing up off the left foot. Even though it starts with the urge to unwind, I feel it moving up my legs through my hips to my chest."

Incredible, I thought. This novice golfer just perfectly described the body's motion in the downswing – something that can take people years of practice to realize, if ever.

"You got it, Sir! There is no difference between that and a golf swing. What else are you feeling?"

"The feeling now is snapping back with my left shoulder which flings my arms and the club."

"Bingo!" I cheered. "Remember the monkey toss? There is a tug of war here: As the club head goes out away from you at a high speed, you have to pull back against that with the handle. You are recruiting your shoulder at the other end of the lever. That's what pulls, with help from the rest of the body and the ground."

"In this week's practice, I recommend you work on your pitching, but pay attention to the monkey toss, as it will carry over to your full swing."

Review of golf lesson:

- The transition starts with the feeling of pressure into the lead foot.

The Memorial Chorten

One block away from my apartment was the Memorial Chorten, a beautiful, powerful structure. I began doing my walking practice around it as often as I could, along with the mostly elder practitioners. They would recite mantras, spin prayer wheels, and one time I saw a gentleman counting his go-arounds by placing a small pebble down on the front step every time he circled. Like Tim Hortons or Dunkin' Donuts, it seemed to be a place for the 'old dogs' to practice and hang out!

Another time I saw a group of elderly women and one really old man, who seemed to be playing the most beautiful Tibetan horn music. The strange thing was, though, he didn't have a horn! All the sounds came out of his mouth. It was stunning, and for an old guy, he had a fabulous set of lungs.

For the first two weeks of my walking practice, every time I did the five minute walk around the chorten, I stubbed my foot and nearly tripped over a

Ed and his Bhutanese brother, Karma Lam.

particular rock that was slightly raised. I would note it but forget the next time around and stumble again and again.

One day I finally managed to keep looking down and not trip over the rock. I looked up triumphantly, only to see a mountain right in front of me that I hadn't noticed before. How can you miss a mountain? It reminded me of that line in the Donovan song: *First there is a mountain, then there is no mountain, then there is.*

That raised rock became a catalyst for the realization that walking meditation is in fact meditation in motion. My everyday awareness was getting stronger.

One day when I walked to the Royal course to meet my juniors, I kept hearing a sound behind me. I assumed it was

"Mr. Duffy lived a short distance from his body."
—James Joyce

85

faster walkers, so I moved to the side, but nobody passed. So I kept walking along and again heard the sound. This time I quickly turned around, but there was nobody there. I assumed the walkers had turned off, so I went back to walking. Again, the sound. It took me a while, but I finally figured out that it was the rustling of my backpack, rubbing when I walked. Classic self-conscious neurosis; something is sneaking up on me from behind. I then realized that the same sound occurred every other day on my walk. I just hadn't noticed it before. I was hearing sounds in my environment that I had missed before practicing meditation.

> "Some of the worst things in my life never happened."
> —Mark Twain

Patrizia and Ugyen

My apartment was owned by a beautiful, fiery Italian woman, Patrizia, and her Bhutanese husband Ugyen Tshering. As the Minister of Labour and Human Resources, Ugyen was one of the most respected and powerful men in Bhutan.

One day he invited me to breakfast to meet my new neighbor, Reba Sobkey, a physician from Los Angeles who had been coming to Bhutan for many years.

The discussion gravitated toward the state of the world today and Bhutan's place on our ever-flattening planet. The country was soon to change from a monarchy to a parliamentary system, much like that of the United Kingdom.

What might be lost when this change happened, we wondered. The King was beloved, and in many ways that loyalty formed the glue for the nation. As separate parties formed, would divisiveness form as well?

We also chatted about the particular magic of Bhutan, something influenced by the predominance of Buddhism. In setting up a new constitution, Ugyen told us, there was an unspoken mandate that this not be lost. It was to be subtly folded into the guidelines for forming this new democracy.

I wondered what lessons Bhutan might learn from other countries, including the US, in setting up this new system.

Monastery.

The country's size alone spoke to this. In Bhutan, everyone knew everyone and what everyone was up to. The King's phone number was listed in the phone book.

There was also the issue of the monastery vote. There are over 14,000 monks and nuns in Bhutan and each one has a vote. That's a powerful block. Monks cannot run for office, but they can certainly influence people. Anybody running for office will have to show their political support for Buddhism.

"The coming of Buddhism to the West may well prove to be the most important event of the Twentieth Century."
—Arnold Toynbee

MONTH THREE

Meditation session – *you* are not your thoughts

Rinpoche and I settled into our positions as usual, but he didn't speak to me. He rang the gong and we sat in meditation. When he rang the gong again, he said softly, "Walking meditation."

This time I was able to keep a steady, slow pace, paying attention to the nuance of my gait. Time seemed to slow down.

He rang the gong again and we sat down.

He finally spoke. "So Ed, this week were you able to keep the consistency of your daily practice?"

I didn't have to think about the answer. "Yes, Sir. In fact it is becoming the most important part of my day!" I offered. "But some sessions I feel like a beginner, with my mind wandering about uncontrollably. I try to touch the thought and go back to the breath, but they keep coming."

His physical appearance seemed to have changed again; today he looked very big.

"There is a story told to me by my teacher: If a dog attacks you and you throw a meaty bone, he will follow the bone. But if a lion attacks and you throw a bone, he won't waver from going straight at you."

"Instead of looking at the thought itself, look at the source of the thought – your mind. Sit with me again, beginning with the regular practice of following the breath. When I ring the gong, contemplate your mind – its location, size, shape, texture, anything that arises."

I settled into an upright posture, firm spine, with my front relaxed. Immediately I saw my mind race to what was becoming a familiar topic: what my life would look like after I left Bhutan.

The gong rang and stopped my reverie. Rinpoche spoke: "Now look for the mind that produces the thoughts."

I started with location. It didn't take long to realize my mind was not just in my head. In fact, I couldn't even be sure it was fully in my body. It wasn't residing in just one spot. A bird was singing outside the window – for a brief instant my mind was out there! But I then a thought arose saying, that's impossible; can't be true.

That there was a mind present was undeniable. But it wasn't anywhere and yet it was everywhere, and I couldn't even call it mine. My thoughts were not my mind, but they arose from mind. Could I deduce that my thoughts arose from nowhere?

The gong rang again. "So Ed, were you able to locate your mind, the source of your thoughts?"

I recounted my inner experience to him that my mind had no location, no form to speak of. "Sir, I could say that my mind doesn't exist, yet it is always present. How can that be?"

"Start looking at your thoughts in that manner," he said in reply. "Be a lion going straight to the source, not a dog chasing a bone of thought. This is called contemplation. It is different from meditation, which has more form, constantly coming back to the breath."

He told me to add a few minutes of contemplation to my daily practice.

Once again, the sound vibrations of the closing gong lasted a very long time.

"A helpful technique for being less attached to your thoughts is to pretend they are coming from the person sitting next to you."
—Dan Harris, author of *10% Happier* and a well-known TV anchor. He finds when he does this practice, that he thinks "What an ...hole he is."

Review of meditation session:

• Consider your thoughts as not necessarily your own.

Golf lesson – pressure into the ground

"Rinpoche, building on the body motion from last week, show me a no-hands swing, with your arms folded in front of you," I began our lesson.

"I hope you are beginning to see the natural quality of that motion. Turn back to the inside of the left heel, push into the front leg and unwind with the monkey toss."

He did it.

"Good," I said. "Now let's add your arms back in. If your arms are relaxed enough, they will be directed by the body motion down and through the ball. We may need to make some adjustments around the path of your hands and club coming down, but those will be minor. Hit a few shots for me, Rinpoche."

He went right back to his shoulders-first, top-down downswing. The ball addiction was still lingering. He still hadn't made the switch to 'swing the club, not hit the ball'.

I was honest with him about his not 'getting it' and decided to try something that had helped many others.

"Key in on one part of the process: the upper body, chest and rib cage, and in particular your left shoulder," I said. "In the backswing, the shoulder moves down and across – that part you is doing really well. In the transition, I suggest you feel like your left shoulder is staying lower longer, as in the frisbee toss. As you do, simultaneously feel your left wrist bowing; again the frisbee feel. At the pro level, the bowing is an effect of other forces. But at your level it can be a conscious motion."

I had him take some practice swings, turning his eyes to the right to watch the space in which his arms needed to travel. "When you swing, your eyes are looking forward at the ball, and golfers don't realize the space that the arms, hands and club need to pass through enroute to the ball," I told him. "When your right shoulder moves outward or is too level, it is invading the space that the arms and club need to pass through. Give it a try."

Being a golf teacher has challenges, but they are far outweighed by the successes. The sound of impact on his next swing was unmistakable: like air being let out of a tire. The ball flew on a perfect trajectory, with a hint of a draw. I calculated that it flew over 150 yards, a fine 7-iron. This student was ready to learn to score.

"Next week Sir, we will meet back on the course. Thank you for your efforts."

> **Review of golf lesson:**
>
> • In the all-important transition, feel the target shoulder low simultaneous to the pressure going into the lead foot.

Meditation session – feeding your demons

After we settled onto our meditation cushions, Rinpoche spoke. "Last time we worked on the course, I mentioned to you that we would be doing an ancient practice, but new to you, that digs deeper into your struggle with the yips. It's called 'Feeding the Demons.' It can be done with any obstacle to your practice or a place in your life where you are stuck."

"A demon takes the energy that you could have access to and freezes it, turning it into a roadblock," he continued. "This practice turns your demons into allies. It is the opposite of our normal way of avoiding or battling problems. Instead, you move toward what you would normally be afraid of. Feeding, not fighting."

First, he said, is to discover where the demon resides in your body. "Do a body scan from head to toe; feel where you hold your yips."

"Notice if the demon there has color or temperature," he said.

"Next, give it shape and texture and move it out of your body to a being or shape out in front of you. Then ask it: What do you want? How will you feel when you get what you need?"

"Then change places with the demon; become the being that represents your yips. Get up and stand in its

"When the resistance is gone, so are the demons."
—Milarepa

91

place. Then answer the questions you just asked it. Once you have done that, come back to your seat. And give the demon what it wants – feed it. Send out your whole being, in the form of nectar-like light, to the demon. Emptying yourself out completely, send the demon everything you've got. Feed it to complete satisfaction."

"It will then disappear, or morph into something else. If it morphs, ask it: 'Are you the ally?' If it answers no, invite the ally to appear."

"Ask the ally some questions: 'How will you help me? How will you protect me? How can I access you?' Then again as before, get up and change places with the ally, and answer these questions. If you get stuck, if nothing arises as an ally, ask yourself: 'If it did arise, what would it look like?' Then dissolve, resting in that state of awareness we have talked about."

"During this whole process, it is critical that you do not get lost in thoughts, but keep it in your body, as a physical feeling. Demons can be like the Hydra of mythology – if you cut off one head, another arises to take its place. As you keep with it, the layers will expose themselves."

Rinpoche told me to do this demon work after my regular sitting meditations. "Next week you will do a guided session with me."

We bowed to each other and I left the room encouraged that there was another way to get at the monster in my golf game.

Lama Tsultrum Allione has brought the ancient Tibetan practice of feeding your demons to the modern world.

https://www.taramandala.org

Review of meditation session:

- Feeding one's demons is an ancient Tibetan practice that enables one to directly confront and neutralize obstacles.

Golf lesson – keep the trail shoulder moving

It was another pristine morning in the Kingdom of Bhutan. As I finished walking up the hill to the world's highest driving range, I couldn't believe what I saw. Rinpoche was already warming up and apparently had gone from slice to hook overnight, as his misses were going left, not high right. Highly unusual.

My young student was accelerating the normal evolution of a golfer's game at the speed of light.

I could only attribute the rapid change to dream yoga, as he was away teaching in Thailand the previous week.

He was hitting big, looping hooks, with as much right-to-left curve as he had hit left-to-right two weeks before. His backswing was full, loaded and powerful. But coming down, his hands were dropping too vertically and for too long. This meant that his hands had to catch up, moving out to the ball sharply, making his hips pitch forward to allow that to happen. If the clubface was open, it was a block/fade; if closed, a sharp low hook, finishing 40 yards off line.

But there was good news, too. He was busting it.

When a student does exactly what I ask, and in fact overdoes it, my first response is elation. But then there's sometimes a hint of embarrassment when I need to inform them that what I said wasn't quite right. In this case, we needed to back up: Rinpoche's right shoulder was stalling, causing a 'slide-slap', meaning his hips were sliding, causing him to slap at the ball with his hands.

"Sir, we need to make some adjustments," I said. "A while back I suggested that you keep your left shoulder low coming down and to drop your arms. That was to get rid of the over-the-top move that resulted in pulls with the shorter clubs and slices with the longer ones. We used the dried-up sod to get your swing inside-out. But now, your pendulum has swung too far from the inside."

I was reminded of a story told by Harvey Penick of his first lesson with a very young Ben Crenshaw. He asked Ben to chip a ball onto the green, which he did. Then, handing him a putter, he asked Ben to knock it into the hole. To which Ben responded: "Why didn't you tell me to do that in the first place!"

I believe that golfers need to know both sides of the coin, in order to self-correct to the middle.

I demonstrated how the club has two ends: grip and club head. Assuming the club is in the right place when parallel to the ground approaching impact, the handle has to move left to get the head moving to the right. The path of the head is still from the inside, but in a way that promotes gradual squaring of the face, rather than a rapid flick.

"Rinpoche, both the frisbee throw and monkey toss have this element. You just need to get your hands moving a little more outward starting the downswing. Stop thinking: 'Left shoulder low, last-minute monkey toss,' to a feeling of unwinding your chest earlier, keeping your hands up a little longer. The key is to unwind on the proper angle, the correct tilt of the shoulders."

I demonstrated by pressing a club against the tips of my shoulders and bent over into a golf posture. Turning back, my left shoulder lowered and went forward as my right one rose and went back behind me. The part of the shaft on my left shoulder pointed just outside the ball.

Coming down, the other side of the club pointed just inside the ball, continuing through until I was fully unwound.

"Sir, imagine there is a clubface on your right shoulder. Hit the ball with that. Keep it going, never stop turning."

I had him try it, moving him through manually the first time. Not surprisingly, he picked it up quickly. "Now, let the turning of the chest move the arm, as opposed to staying wound up and letting the arms drop," I instructed. "Feel like you are leaving your arms behind."

I had him swing to the top and stop. I walked in and held a hand on the butt of his club. "Can you start down without pushing on my hand with the club?"

He made a few practice swings. He was starting from the ground up much better.

"Ed, it feels more like the frisbee toss than before, I feel the pressure of my left pec on my left arm much earlier," he said.

Bobby Jones was asked if he could distill what his swing feels like.

He answered, "I feel like I'm leaving my arms behind."

94

He struggled with the timing when hitting balls; his smooth swing became jerky. And he tended to unwind his shoulders too level.

"Sir, I am confident that you understand this move, you just need to get familiar with it. Practice this week to make it smoother, accelerating gradually rather than quickly. And do the drill with the club on your shoulders to get the right amount of tilt."

"Thanks once again for your efforts, Rinpoche."

Review of golf lesson:

- To neutralize a club that comes into the ball from too much inside, turn the torso while leaving the arms behind.

Meditation session – what color is your demon?

Sitting facing my spiritual friend, I had the thought that, as hard as golf is, understanding my demons was even harder. Just like the Hydra metaphor Rinpoche mentioned, they seemed to have 100 heads; cut one off and another grew back in its place. Now, he seemed to be able to read my thoughts.

"Ed, you have worked on feeding the demon for a week now, do you have any questions on that process?"

"Yes," I said. "When I look for my mind before thought, it feels like the demons get stronger."

He asked me to describe that to him.

"Under the yips demon is a much larger, deeper one," I said. "I keep going back to a difficult time in my life. I had an idyllic childhood in a rural, safe and friendly place. I had many friends and enjoyed more than anything taking long walks following a winding stream with my dog."

"Before we moved, I saw the world as friendly and inviting," I continued. "Moving from that place at the critical

"Demons take the energy you could have access to. Move toward that which you would naturally be afraid of. Then the demon becomes your ally."

"Feeding, not fighting."

—Tsultrim Allione at a conference in Boulder, Colorado

age of puberty, to a place I perceived as mean and unfeeling, made me with-drawn and lacking confidence. I began to believe the world was tough and unfair."

I told him that I did everything I could to escape that feeling, eventually covering it over with an obsession with golf. It was a huge band-aid. My only friends became golfers.

Rinpoche listened intently, then spoke: "The fact that you can name it is the first step in softening and moving through it," he began. "What I am about to tell you will probably shock you, just as much of your wisdom in golf has shocked me: Sadness is very good news. It is a pathway to the warrior's mind."

"However, as you have discovered, it is too painful to stick with the sadness unless you realize facing it directly is what you have learned to do in your meditation practice. And surely if you label that sadness as bad, you will be stuck. As I said, sadness is the warrior's mind. Sadness brings delight."

"In doing this demon practice, start small, with demons that are not over-powering. First learn the process before going deeper. You have discovered that the yips are a tentacle of the deeper problem. But start with the smaller defilement – the yips, before tackling anything bigger."

When he said this, I felt relief. My yips, my obsession, suddenly seemed like less of a big deal.

Rinpoche said he would guide me through a session, but that we should sit for 10 minutes first. "Feeding the demon work is impossible without being able to keep your mind in one place for an extended period," he said.

We sat together and then he spoke: "So the obstacle I want you to feed is the yips. Staying in meditation posture, see if you can locate the feeling asso-ciated with this demon, where does it live in your body?"

He gave me lots of space, as I went deep inside myself looking for the yips. It was a twitchy feeling, skittish, and it resided in my shoulders and hands. On closer look, it was also in my neck. It was as if I had no feeling from my chest down.

"Does it have a color, a texture?" Rinpoche prompted.

"It feels twitchy and fearful, like a hyperactive squirrel," I told him after a few moments.

"Can you make it solid and put it outside yourself?" he then asked.

At first the external image was vague, but I could see it taking shape slowly in front of me. It was a skinny, slightly transparent man-squirrel, constantly twitching. And it was very unstable, with one very thin leg. It was slowly wobbling in front of me, off balance and scared.

"Ask what it wants," Rinpoche said softly.

It dawned on me that I wasn't talking, or at least I don't remember talking. He seemed to just know when to ask the next question. I made a mental note to ask him how he did that.

For now I spoke out loud to the image in front of me. "What do you want? What do you need?"

I sat for a good while, waiting for an answer.

Rinpoche, again speaking very softly, guided me. "Now get up from your cushion and sit on the demon's cushion. Become the demon. When an answer comes, voice it."

It took a long time for me to put into words the feeling I had as the yips. It was unbalanced yet strangely powerful. "I need to be perfect. I need to be the best. Otherwise the pain I felt when I was 13 will come back. You won't love me unless you see me as perfect."

These words came from a place in me that was a bit scary – some hidden, wounded place I hadn't visited in a long time.

Rinpoche spoke then: "Good. Now come back to your cushion and give the demon what it wants."

I moved back to my original seat but found a great deal of resistance trying to send love to my long time nemesis. Eventually that softened into feeling sorry for this mis-shaped, needy part of me. For a moment the demon became a little baby that I wanted to cradle in my arms. I began to send a loving beam of light out to it. I imagined myself slowly disappearing as the good stuff left me and went to the sorry-looking twitch-thing.

I finally disappeared completely. The demon then changed into a pendulum, like a metronome used by musicians. The beat was soothing, steady.

"Ask it if it is your ally," I heard my teacher say.

"Are you my ally?" I asked, already knowing the answer. It answered yes. I remembered the instructions from last week and needed no prompt.

"How will you help me and protect me?"

I got up and sat again in the other cushion, this time belonging to my ally.

"I will help you bring stability and steadiness to your putting. My steady rhythm is always available. If you ever have trouble finding me, look for your own heartbeat."

Rinpoche spoke again: "Now dissolve yourself, resting in the mind before thoughts."

At that moment, rather than retreating to a faraway place, I felt completely present in this moment. "Thank you Rinpoche," was all I could say.

Review of meditation session:

- Feel the demon in your body, give it shape and texture, put it outside yourself, find out what it wants. Feed it completely then find your ally.

Golf lesson – two chips

I woke up to a dusting of snow, which was unusual in Thimphu. (When it does snow, it's a celebration and the schools and hospitals close.) It didn't stick, though and it became a beautiful day by 9:00 am. I ran into the chief surgeon on the course. "I feel bad – had to cancel two surgeries," he said.

In Bhutan work is not always priority #1! Maybe that's why it's called the Happy Kingdom.

Rinpoche drove up wearing a maroon golfing shirt, the same color as his robes. Even though the course was busy because of the holiday, the putting and pitching practice green was vacant.

I dropped a few balls around the green in various lies and situations. "Sir, at this stage of your game, you need to know three main shots: low with little spin, low with plenty of spin, and high with medium spin," I began.

I explained that the low no-spin is from just off the green, in a place where you can't putt because the grass in front would be impossible to judge. It is one of the easiest shots in golf, called the 'putt-chip'.

"Does meditation help your golf, or does golf help your meditation?"
—Melvin McLeod, Editor, *The Lions Roar*

I told him he'd be using his 6-iron as a putter. "Hold it very much up and down and hold it as you would a putter," I said. "Your wrists will be arched and the heel of the club will be off the ground."

We had briefly touched upon this shot in an earlier lesson.

Rinpoche gave me a quizzical look, something I got often when teaching this. There are a number of reasons for the club not lying flat, I explained and perhaps most important is that arched wrists eliminate flippy wrists.

"Now just swing it like a putter," I told him. "The only way you can mess up is to add a lift to the swing. Trust the loft – it will get up just the right amount. Remember, it isn't a high shot."

There aren't many ways to mess up this shot. One would be the arc being too deep or too high relative to the ground. "Cut the grass right at the roots for the correct depth," I guided him.

The second way would be by putting the bottom of the arc in the wrong place. "It can be just past the ball," I said, something we had worked on before.

I had him make 20 or so practice swings to get these two non-negotiables in place, then to try the same with a ball. His contact was fine, which is the most important point.

"Now, Sir, notice how far the ball rolls out." I measured in paces the amount of carry from where the ball started to where it landed on the green. "Five paces. Now starting here, I will walk off the amount of roll."

I ended at 30 paces. "Six-to-one ratio on a flat green. This is surprisingly consistent," I said. "Want it to roll less? Hit a 9-iron." This would result in a three-to-one ratio.

I had him hit several shots to different targets. As usual, he caught on quickly.

"Well done!" I said. "Next, the low spinner."

I told him this shot would be used from a little further out, especially when the lie is less than perfect. "The club leans a little more forward at address, back to your normal grip and lower hands. The key is to strike the ball with the club still forward leaning. In order to do that, your chest needs to turn a little through the shot."

As typical when I teach this shot, his hands separated from his body in the follow-through. "Rinpoche, remember the feeling of left pec on left triceps?

99

Same feeling here. At impact the hands are done working, just add a little turn of the body to finish."

I told him we would tackle the high shot at a later date. "See you tomorrow."

Review of golf lesson:

- On the putt chip use high arched hands. The pitching wedge ratio is one in the air to two on the ground, air time to roll time. 9-iron=3-1, 8 iron=4-1, 7-iron=5-1, and so on. This shot works well with a hybrid!
- The spin chip requires a forward-leaning shaft, and a slight body turn-through.

Meditation session – quiet eyes

"Let's sit together for 10 minutes," Rinpoche said, signaling the start of our next session.

Meditation today felt like a refreshing swim in a lake. Even the sound of the gong as it faded away was delightful.

"Ed, the physical motion of golf is not a concept," Rinpoche began. "It is accomplished by the senses. Feel and sight are the main ones."

"Sit with me for another session. The first time I instructed you on this practice I mentioned your eyes, softly gazing, resting in one spot."

"Notice if your eyes are resting in one place, unwavering, or if they are jumping around. Resting is different than staring; there will be no strain if your eyes are soft. The practice is not looking at something, but rather paying attention to the way you are looking."

"Start as always settling into your sense of feel, your rear on the cushion, your hands on your thighs, the air on your face. Then to the eyes."

After resting in the feeling of being there, I noticed my eyes settling on a slight discoloration on the rug. It was the

Gary McCord spoke in a video he made that discussed the teachings of Mac O'Grady. He spoke of the foveal field covering the ball and its surroundings all through the swing. Neck tilt serves to enable foveal view all the time. Thus, **foveal** vision may also be defined as the central 1.5–2° of the **field** of vision.

first time I had ever paid attention to the act of looking, rather than what I looked at. And it was impossible to gaze softly for more than a few seconds, without the focus changing slightly, in and out, and then drift around the object. Keeping my eyes soft felt like making them quiet. The only way I could keep my gaze in one place was when it felt like the mark on the rug was actually inside of me. The quietness then became easy and natural.

When the session ended, Rinpoche asked if I had any questions.

"I do, sir. Do you think this practice could be applied to golf?"

"Absolutely," he replied. "The notion of resting eyes comes from the ancient kyudo, or Zen archery practice. I had the good fortune to practice with Shabata Sensei, who was part of an unbroken lineage of 20 generations of bow-makers to the emperor of Japan. Even at a very advanced age, he could still demonstrate incredible accuracy with the bow."

The eyes are obviously very important in reading the greens, but other senses can blend together. I have heard Nick Price say. "Feel the pace with your eyes."

During a Golf Channel Playing Lesson, Paula Creamer also said, "Feel it with your eyes."

Review of meditation session:

- Resting eyes means resting mind.
- When the master golf teacher Harvey Penick gave last-minute words of advice to students before big events, he would often say "use your eyes."

Patience practice

"I learned patience, Dad."

—Katie Hanczaryk, when asked what she learned after four months of volunteer work in Bhutan.

Things in Bhutan do not happen at the speed Westerners are accustomed to. 'Open at 9', for example, is not a sure thing. I experienced this one morning when I walked down

Katie at a festival.

to my favorite little coffee shop only to find it wasn't open yet. So to kill some more time, I walked to the great outdoor coliseum/sports field in the middle of town.

When I got there, I realized my mind had gone back to the impatience theme I had noticed in my meditations, constantly trying to fill time by thinking or doing stuff. If I were truly patient, I thought, I could just be.

I took a seat on the solid rock structure and decided to see what 15 minutes of just being felt like. I didn't meditate, daydream, contemplate, plan, or anything. I just sat there. And sat, and sat, and be'd, and be'd.

Many times I wanted to get up and do something. But I stuck with the plan. I had been meditating in the traditional way for many months, but this practice went right to the core of my impatience.

A phrase I'd heard from Rinpoche came to mind: "Only

"We are human beings, not human doings."
—The Adventures of Buckaroo Banzai Across the 8th Dimension

from the state of being can you do great things. Doing without being has no legs to stand on."

After 15 minutes I stood up. I felt calm, and the Serenity Prayer came to me: *Lord grant me the serenity to accept the things I cannot change; courage to change the things I can; and wisdom to know the difference.*

Heading back to see if the coffeeshop had opened, I smiled thinking of the great golfer of a bygone era, Walter Hagen, who said, "Don't worry, don't hurry, and don't forget to smell the flowers along the way."

Golf lesson – where *he* teaches *me* how to putt

Rinpoche and Karma were on the putting green when I arrived. He called me over.

"Ed, you have not spoken in our lessons on how to use my eyes," he said. "I have experimented this week on using the resting gaze in my golf and have found it profoundly effects my ability to perform." He seemed excited about his new discovery.

"Would you mind if I gave you a putting lesson?"

"Wow," I replied, "no problem. But don't expect me to give you meditation instruction!"

"Ed," he said, "look at the ball in a different way. Not too tight, not too loose, but steady. Let your eyes rest on a dimple, any one. If you are too tight, that would be staring. In meditation that leads to headaches. If too loose, you are not fully engaged."

I stood over a 5-foot putt with my old Scotty Cameron putter, doing my best to follow his instruction.

"Sir, I am finding my eyes flicker after a few seconds. But if I loosen up a bit, they go back to resting."

He nodded. "The point is not only resting eyes but having your mind on feeling where the hole is. If the mind is also on the ball, the gaze becomes too tight. Look at the hole with the same resting eye. Then back to the ball. Resting, not darting around. Your mind is on the memory of the hole. It is of course a memory, since you are no longer looking at it."

I tried it: Rest on the hole, then the ball, mind on the hole. Then I pulled the trigger and knocked it into the center of the cup. I remembered reading how Tiger Wood's father, Earl, taught him to 'putt to the picture'.

We spent the whole session putting from different distances.

"Look at the hole with quiet, resting eye," Rinpoche instructed, "then let your mind expand out; eyes still on the hole but seeing also what is around the hole with an open focus. Small expands out to big, then slowly back again to small."

In Bhutan they say contemplating death five times daily brings happiness.

I was draining putts from all over, but my excitement was tempered by a familiar worry: Could I do it on the course, under pressure?

"Ed, tomorrow I will be performing a *Sukhavadi* ritual for a monk who died yesterday, a ceremony where all the monks meditate in the room with the body." I had the thought of how different our culture is around death, keeping it hidden.

He went on, "Let's say today was a meditation session as well as a golf lesson, I'll see you next week."

"Thanks for the lesson, Rinpoche," I answered.

Review of golf lesson:

- The quiet eye is a resting gaze, not a stare.

Golf session – tug-of-war

Golf is not an easy game. In fact, for some it verges on impossible. Look at the swing of basketballer Charles Barkley. Now substitute the word 'lurch' in place of 'swing'.

When I approached the range I heard the deeply unsatisfying sound of an iron being hit off the hosel. When the young monk saw me, however, his face didn't show frustration, but curiosity.

"Pro, yesterday I hit the ball very well in practice," he began right away. "But today I seem to be topping or hitting way off the toe, so much that the ball is shooting off to the right."

I had a roll of painter's tape in my teaching bag and took it out. I put a strip of tape across the clubface, from toe to heel. He hit the first shot pretty well, but when we looked at the mark on the tape from the impact with the ball, it was clearly on the heel side.

"Hit another," I requested.

This time I had to jump back quickly as the ball shot straight right. Before we looked at the tape, I asked him to guess where on the clubface it hit. He said he thought it had hit off the toe based on where it went. "But strangely it didn't feel that way," he added.

When we looked, the clear mark of the dimples was imprinted on the hosel. A classic shank.

"Rinpoche, among some golfers 'shank' is a dirty word, not allowed to be spoken out loud," I told him. "Once they start, they can stick around for a long time. I have known people who have quit the game because of that nasty shot."

"Months ago, when we started this process, you were prone to hit shots on the hosel as well, but for a very different reason: your club went out and away from you early in the downswing, over the top. You fixed that problem quickly, when you went from slice to hook."

"But now, you are coming too much from behind, and moving your hands outward too late in the swing."

In the motion of swinging, I said, there is an outward force pulling the club away from you. "You need to learn to offset that with an inward force," I said. "Back home the kids play a game called tug-of-war. It's like that."

I asked him to hold the club in his left hand, belt high, and level to the ground. I stood facing him and held the other end of the club in my left hand. Then I asked him to see if he could pull the handle straight back, out of my hand.

"There are four ways you can pull me," I said. "Two are wrong, one is OK, one is ideal."

The first way is to allow the force of pulling to lift your hand to line up with the shaft. "That way is wrong," I told him. "Keep your hand down."

The second wrong way is to just lean backward on your heels. If I were to let go of my end, I told him, you would stumble backward.

The next move, partially correct, is to bend the left elbow, using your arm muscles only. Some very good golfers use this technique in conjunction with the best way, which is keeping the hand down at belt height and turning the chest, thereby pulling the club straight back.

"Let's play tug of war, try to pull me over," I said.

On the first attempt, he was just leaning back. I let go of my end, and he staggered backward, startling his ever-present attendant Karma.

The next try he got the idea of turning and pulling. But with my experience of using the earth and being settled into a low center of gravity, I won easily by pulling him forward.

Gradually, he got it and we played to a tie. But his hands were rising from their original lower starting position.

"That is the feeling of using inward force, Rinpoche. Now add in the proper grip by putting the club more across and in your fingers."

During the next round of tug-of-war, I told him, maintain that angle between your left arm and the club.

Again, I pulled him over easily at first, but once he got the hang of the grip more in his fingers he was able to match me. He even knocked me off balance once.

"That move, Rinpoche, will not only stop your shank, it will also add a new level of precision and power in your ball striking."

I had him hit a few short shots focusing on the feeling of pulling the handle straight back.

But now a different problem emerged: The level-to-the-ground shoulder turn up as we just did the tug of war exercise had to become tilted as he bent over into the address position.

At first, he was turning-through too level, causing thin and otherwise poorly struck shots. But once we got the tilt right, the shank was gone.

I had him hit some full shots with a wedge. Every third

"We stumble and fall constantly, even when we are most enlightened."
—Thomas Merton

The students are watching closely.

or fourth was 'pured', and the others were close. His swing was evolving, but it was missing one very important piece, the glue that pulls it together and makes it consistent: Rhythm.

Review of golf lesson:

• Don't be fooled by a shot with an iron that shoots off to the right. Your logic suggests a strike off the toe of the club, when in fact it's right off the heel, on that protruding bump called the hosel.

MONTH FOUR

Meditation session – dream yoga

Jack Nicklaus had a dream the night before the final round of the US Open. It was about his grip; the next day he went out with the grip change and played great, winning the event.

"Ed, you asked me a while back about dream yoga. You are at a point where you could begin the process of learning this practice," Rinpoche told me the next time I saw him.

He said it would take awhile to get to the place where I could use the practice how I wanted, even in my dreams, but that I was ready for the preliminary steps.

"Tonight, when you are going to bed, put a notebook and pencil on your bedside table," he said. "If you wake up in the middle of the night or in the morning and you remember a dream, write it down. If you set the intention before bed that you are going to remember dreams, it won't be long until you do. The most advantageous time for dreaming is just before you wake up in the morning, when you are half awake," he added.

A golf swing takes around a second. Twenty-seven shots, with no time in between for walking, would take half a minute!

I was curious about how he used this practice. "Sir, when you do this yoga, what are you actually doing, how does it work?"

"This is first and foremost a spiritual practice, a way to deepen your practice by getting to know the hidden parts of your mind," he explained. "It extends the number of hours one can practice. But it is also a time to do pretty much anything you want. Many of my Western students at first use it to make love to the literal man or woman of their dreams."

"Another attraction at first is flying, which can be quite

exhilarating. But once the initial thrill has worn off, it can be a time to develop on many levels."

I knew what I wanted to do with it. "So how do you use it for learning golf? Obviously, it has fast-forwarded your learning curve. I have never had a student come along so quickly!"

"Ed, I review what you and I worked on in our last session and I hit balls visualizing the swing you are teaching me. Then I hit some doing it wrong. I want to know the difference. And even though I am lying down in bed, asleep, I can totally feel the swing. I then go out and play as many holes as I can before waking up. Last night I shot 27 for nine holes. Mind you, I can fly between shots, so it only took a few minutes!"

This was to me an Alice in Wonderland moment – consciously playing golf in your dreams was something I had never heard of. I was almost expecting him to break into laughter and say 'gotcha!', but his facial expression remained very matter-of-fact.

"But," he continued, "I also have some bad ball-striking rounds, working on my scrambling. The thing is, you can direct your own reality, as there are no physical restraints."

He told me to keep with my daily meditation practice, but to work on recalling my dreams in the coming week.

So far along with a daily meditation practice, I also had walking meditation, as well as contemplation practice. And now dream yoga; my practice was expanding!

Review of meditation session:

- The first step in dream yoga is remembering your dreams.

Golf lesson – tempo

As Rinpoche hit some warm-up irons, there was still some major inconsistency, which my trained eye saw as varying swing speeds, or changing relationships, between the back and downswing.

"Rinpoche, today we will not be talking about positions or body parts. Instead we will discuss the flow, the rhythm of a swing. There is a story of the great player from Texas, Byron Nelson. One morning before an event, he was having breakfast at a diner, when the 'Merry Widow Waltz' came on the jukebox. He played an incredible round, which he directly attributed to having the waltz playing in his head."

"Can you sing it to me, Ed?"

In my warbling, off-key voice, I belted it out.

I explained to him that the beat/rhythm/meter of a waltz is 123-1, 123-1. An effective golf swing has a 3-1 back-swing- to-downswing ratio for a driver. (Irons average 2.5-1, putting is 2-1).

He thought about that for a while. As he did, the sound of the monks doing their daily chants drifted by. He began chanting along with them:

Om Mani Padme Hum,
Om Mane Padme Hum

It was something I'd heard often during my time in Bhutan, called the mantra of the compassionate *Chenrezig*, and is said to contain all the teachings of the Buddha.

In this prayer I could hear our needed tempo: 123-1, 123-1. 'Om' was the forward press. 'Mani padme' was the backswing, 'Hum', the downswing to impact.

"Sir, hit some shots with that cadence, backswing to downswing. Don't forget the subtle forward press to begin the motion."

He told me then that he had an interview with a British newspaper so had to leave early, before adding: "I will be practicing tonight and will have it by next week."

I couldn't help but bow to him. Even the golf lessons were becoming a spiritual teaching.

Tibetan Buddhists believe that saying the mantra (prayer), *Om Mani Padme Hum*, out loud or silently to oneself, invokes the powerful benevolent attention and blessings of *Chenrezig*, the embodiment of compassion.

Viewing the written form of the mantra is said to have the same effect — it is often carved into stones, and placed where it can be seen.

Review of golf lesson:

• Swing tempo, driver count: three backswing, one downswing. Irons are two-and-a-half to one, putting is two to one.

Meditation session

As always, we started the session with a deep bow and a short period of meditation. After the sound of the gong faded, he asked me if I had any questions.

"Sir, I am remembering pieces of dreams," I told him. "I see what you mean about the power of setting the intention to remember. It works."

"Good," he replied. "As I said, that is the first step to using dreams to further your understanding."

"Next you need to learn how to wake up within the dream," he continued. "In your waking state, if you jump up, you will always come back down to earth. But in a dream if you jump you might keep going up and begin to fly, or you might bounce when you land, like on a trampoline. In the Buddhist tradition, even our waking state is considered a dream, but that's for a later discussion."

"For now, your practice is to differentiate between the awake and dream states. During the day, ask yourself many times: 'Is this a dream?' The answer can be found if you do a little hop. If you land normally, it's not a dream. If the landing is odd, and you are aware of that, then you are lucid dreaming."

I took that all in and tried to imagine myself actually doing it. "Rinpoche, I might feel silly hopping if people are around," I said. "Is there another way to check?"

"There are many ways. You can simply look at your hand. If it changes in size, or any number of odd things begin to happen, you will also know: dream or awake. As soon as you realize you are dreaming, you are in! The next step is learning to direct the dream as you wish."

"Please understand," he continued, "this is not a parlor trick or a way to indulge your fantasies. Traditionally it is powerful training for the *bardo*, that space between dying and being reborn. When you die, your senses begin to dissolve. They fade out one by one until nothing is left but

Dream Yoga is one of the six yogas of Naropa. Naropa was an Indian *Mahasidda*, a disciple of Tilopa.

your mind, which is pure awareness. Holding on, or attaching yourself to what no longer exists, destines you to be reborn in unfortunate realms. Dream yoga is a practice to prevent that."

"Ed, I will be teaching in Thailand next week. Good luck in your practice until we meet again." We shook hands. "Safe travels," I said as we parted.

Walking outside, I did a little hop…landing firmly. Not dreaming, I thought to myself. The rest of the day I hopped many times, asking the question "Is this a dream?"

Review of meditation session:

- Hop or look at your hand to wake up in a dream.

Playing

I was able to play a few times that week that he was gone, both after teaching the juniors and on my days off. Often I would play with a few of the juniors or club members I had befriended.

A pattern began to emerge. I would invariably start out playing well, no yips, relaxed ball striking. Then around the seventh hole, just as it looked like I would put together a good scoring round, the yips would come back. And as the round progressed that yippy, tight feeling would bleed into my full swing.

"Let things happen and be the ball."
—Ty Webb, Caddyshack

My meditation practice had gotten stronger, to a point where it began to impact my life off the cushion. I was able to watch my mind as a negative state began to rise. And I could definitely see this in my game. There was a tipping point where relaxation and trust in my skill turned into wanting a good score too much. It always seemed to occur around the seventh hole. Rinpoche had talked before about the basic problem of human existence – the root of all suffering: grasping. That lesson was becoming clear to me.

Round after round, a great start devolved into a rough middle. Then once the round was blown, I gave up wanting it so badly and started playing well again. Mental note: Ask my spiritual friend how to stay on this side of the tipping point. Though in my heart, I knew what his answer would be: "Just stay with it, embody it, be curious about it and then come back to the breath."

That night, I doubled down on my intention to remember my dreams – and to remember to hop. I had had a full day of teaching with the juniors and was very tired, so it wasn't long before I fell sound asleep.

I woke up around midnight with a strong feeling left over from a dream, but I couldn't remember any of the details. The feeling was one of sadness. My meditation practice had evolved to the point where, rather than ignoring or pushing away feelings, I would just let them be, experiencing them fully. Oddly, the sadness had some joy underneath it.

Before dozing off again, I again set the intention to remember and to explore waking up within the dream.

Just before dawn, I found myself on the range at Royal Thimphu Golf Club with the juniors. The mountains looked impossibly high and closer than I had remembered them. Suddenly, from the very top of a mountain, a huge bird swooped down. On the bird, riding it like a horse, was Rinpoche.

Then I remembered to hop. And I began to fly, floating alongside the bird and my teacher. It was exhilarating; I didn't want it to stop. Rinpoche turned to me and said: "Now it's time to do something meaningful."

I woke up to a feeling new to me – a calmness that lasted all day. I had experienced my first lucid dream.

That week the flying dreams came nearly every night, always accompanied by a feeling of bliss. I couldn't wait to tell Rinpoche the good news.

"When you fall asleep every night, you're actually falling awake - into a dimension of reality that's as vast as the cosmos." —Andrew Holecek *Dream Yoga*

Meditation session – hope and fear

The gong rang and we settled into our sitting practice. My mind was agitated, though, as I had two pressing matters I wanted to discuss with Rinpoche. First, I wanted to tell him the good news of the dream. And second, about the pattern of losing it on the course.

"Ed, do you have anything you would like to discuss?"

I was never very good at hiding my inner world – it always came out in my body language. He knew I had lots on my mind. I was probably squirming on the meditation cushion.

"Rinpoche, two things: First, I had my first awake dream. Once I realized I was dreaming, taking control of it didn't seem too hard. By the way, you were in the dream and you gave me some advice to do something meaningful."

"Ed, you will be able to access your dreams more frequently now that you know how," he said. "The next step is to set the intention to follow my advice. What to work on depends on many things."

"Before deciding on that, what is your second question? Perhaps they are connected."

"Sir, I can start a round with a relaxed, steady putting stroke. But as the round progresses, I tighten up. That tightness expands from putting to the full swing and I end up hitting some god-awful shots."

"Describe the difference between the early round and the later tightness," he asked.

"It feels like I realize how well I am doing, how good it feels and how much I want it to continue. It's at that point that it begins to slip through my fingers."

He settled back on his cushion for a moment. "Ed, the emotion of fear can manifest in many ways. It is connected intimately with wanting something, as you say. Wanting it and the fear of losing it are the same thing. Let's do some demon work around that fear."

Buddhism is a nontheistic religion. The Buddha on his deathbed said to his students: "Therefore, O Ananda, be ye lamps unto yourselves. Rely on yourselves, and so not rely on external help."

"Hold fast to the truth as a lamp. Seek salvation alone in the truth. Look not for assistance to any one besides yourselves."

We repeated the process we did earlier around the yips. First he had me externalize the fear and strike up a conversation. Then I asked what it wanted. Finally I gave it everything, including myself.

The image that came up was of a toddler with a pacifier, having a tantrum if anybody threatened to take it away. The baby then morphed into a shriveled-up Gollum from Lord of the Rings, disfigured and tragic because of his fear of losing the 'Precious'.

When we were done, Rinpoche told me that I should explore my fear further in my dream.

We bowed to each other and I left hopeful, but also wishing it could be easier. As that thought was forming, I realized that it too was fear.

Review of meditation session:

- Hope and fear, wanting something and fear of losing something, will surely disrupt mindfulness. Notice it and come back to the breath.

Dream

It took a few sleeps but early one morning, while in a dream, I remembered to look at my hand. I realized there were too many fingers and I said to myself: "This is a dream. Now do something meaningful."

Suddenly I saw myself on the first hole of a beautiful golf course. I had the dream caddy, literally – my brother Paul. Paul had died a few years earlier, but when he was alive he was always able to get my mind right on the course.

We had the whole course to ourselves, except for one spectator. Gollum was walking around with us. My first reaction was horror that this perfect day was already ruined, but Paul stepped in.

"Ed, I invited him to come watch. You will play better

A good friend, Ted Stonehouse, is the Director of Golf at the prestigious Cabot Cliffs resort in Cape Breton.

The great Canadian golfer Moe Norman often played at a course where Ted was an apprentice in Ontario.

One day Ted heard Mr. Norman in the golf shop mumbling something under his breath..."Hope and fear, hope and fear."

Ted had to ask, "Sir, what are you saying?" Moe answered, "Hope and fear, hope and fear, big problem!"

with a spectator and you can use his energy. I set some rules for him however. He is not allowed to give you advice or to distract you in any way. Being the only spectator, he has lots of space. He will be with us on every shot – present, but not involved."

As I hit my first tee shot, my body felt powerful and my mind calm. The ball carried over 400 yards and went in for an ace. I woke up incredibly happy, not only to see my brother again, but also with a deep image of how to work with the demon of fear.

Lying awake in bed, I thought about my hard landing from Amherst to Washington as a teenager. On one hand, as trauma goes, it was mild. But the outcome was my grasping onto golf as an escape and my belief that my only way out was to excel at golf. The fear was that, without golf, those feelings of not fitting in and of being confused and unsure of myself would return.

That fear was being covered up, but was always there, escaping in the form of the yips.

Golf session – a friendly round of golf

It was another crystal clear day and Rinpoche and I both had time for nine holes. I went first. The downhill par three was a dartboard for a good player under normal conditions. But it had been dry lately and my well-struck 9-iron landed 10 feet short of the green and took a big bounce to the back.

I saw Rinpoche change clubs, happy that he was 'going to school' on my shot. He went through his routine as I had taught him, but when he approached the ball he did something I had never seen anyone do on the course. It was mesmerizing.

Standing sideways to the target, feet spread wide, he held the club upside down in his left hand, raised his arm to a 45-degree angle, and pointed the butt of the club in the direction of the target. His other arm pointed down 45 degrees, making him look like the Bhutanese archers I had been watching, with a fully loaded bow.

Bhutanese archer.

He looked majestic, frozen there for a few seconds, before addressing the ball. His shot looked good, but I could hear it was hit a little fat. With the extra roll on the fairway, it finished on the front fringe.

"Sir, what was that?" I asked as we walked to the green.

"In the kyudo tradition, the masters can focus the energy of the environment. I am working on developing that skill in my game," he said. "When I feel it is at a point to teach, I will show you."

It was a delightful round of golf, as we had morphed from teacher/student to two friends just playing golf. We were both playing extremely well, and for myself the occasional bad shot didn't bother me, because I could rely on my short game.

On the last green, my caddy Rinchen said something a caddy should never say: "Coach, if you hole this putt, you will tie the course record!"

I hadn't even been aware of my score. The eight foot birdie putt suddenly looked like a rattlesnake about to strike. I tried all the tricks I thought would help – awareness of breath, calling up my ally, quiet eye, even picturing the walking-with-fear dream. Nothing worked.

"Rinpoche, there is no way I can make this," I said.

He smiled. "Next week we will talk about something new: egolessness," he said calmly.

I three putted for a 33. Hardly a score to be dejected about, but it still left a bad taste in my mouth.

Review of golf lesson:

- Two friends playing golf, sharing a beautiful day.

> "Stop the conversation!" —Dr. Joe Parent, (Zen Golf) to Vijay Singh, after he noticed that Vijay and his caddy would talk right up to the ball.
>
> Dr. Parent wanted him to have a focused entry period well in advance.
>
> Vijay went on to become world #1.

Meditation session – egolessness

After our short practice session and a deep bow, Rinpoche began.

"One of the main teachings of the Buddha is called egolessness. To say you don't exist is on one hand a ridiculous statement. Of course you are here, occupying space on this earth. You have thoughts that feel and are real to you. That's called relative truth."

"But that is not the whole enchilada."

He loved using interesting English language phrases. Obviously this one was learned in the US on a teaching tour.

"We once did an exercise of looking for your self," he continued. "If I'm not mistaken, you never found it."

"In the absolute sense, there is no separate self. It is an illusion created by your mind."

A stream of questions arose in my mind: How do I function without a me? Does that mean I shouldn't care anymore? Am I now to be swallowed up by the cosmic soup? Become a jellyfish?

He continued: "We feel that consciousness is ours, separate. In fact, consciousness is everywhere. The consciousness and thoughts, emotions and feelings are only fleeting, only passing through. We want to make things permanent, while if people just looked around with some critical intelligence, they would see that nothing is permanent. It is that freezing of thoughts that causes a sense of separateness, and from that comes the fear. This is a difficult notion to grasp, but it is the essence of enlightenment."

"But sir, how do I move, how do I live without a self?" I asked, a little panicked.

"You live with grace, power and compassion. As you told me early on, in golf you gain control by giving up control," he replied.

My meditation practice was already loosening up my solid sense of self, he said. "You are seeing that thoughts

> "True happiness consists in eliminating the false sense of 'I'."
> —The Buddha

come and go, like the imprint of a bird in the sky."

"Every time you sit, you are noticing thoughts and feelings that come from nowhere – they are not even really yours. You are softening up the boundaries of what you formally thought of as a self. It's still your mind, but it's in a bigger space."

"If there really was a central self, a CEO who's in charge, then he would be in control of your thoughts, feelings, your concepts, even your body. But you are finding that you cannot control those things. And if you really had a self, it would not change through time. Your self as a teenager would be the same as your self now. That simply is not the case."

"I said earlier that awareness is everywhere, but that doesn't mean your self is everywhere. What you think of as you is made up of many different pieces: body, feelings, what you perceive with your five senses, your view of the world and the mind, which can be conscious of all of that. Problems arise when you think all of that is you. The mind consciousness, because it believes the first four pieces are real, gets tangled up in them. The untangled mind is primordially pure. The most direct way to experience this untangling is meditation."

"Ed," he said, "the Tibetan New Year is a time of great celebration in Bhutan and it is coming up next week."

For me this meant a week off from teaching the juniors and for Rinpoche it meant a week of practice with the other monks.

"On the far end of the yak field is a retreat cabin, which won't be in use for that week," Rinpoche said. "A seven day solitary retreat would solidify your practice 100-fold. Would you like to do that?"

My mind raced. A week alone? Meditating all day?

"I do have the time, but it's a scary thought," I admitted. "How does it work?"

"Nothing ever exists entirely alone; everything is in relation to everything else."
—Gautama Buddha

"Spend time alone and you will find your edges."
—Newfoundland saying

Rupa at Taktsang.

"The great meditators of the past did very long retreats. I myself have done a traditional three year retreat in the very cabin you would be in."

"As a newer practitioner, I would suggest a modified schedule: Four one-and-a-half hour sessions throughout the day. Meals will be brought to you, so no time needed to cook or clean up."

"And bring your clubs and shag bag. Both for exercise and to deepen your golf practice. I would suggest two one-hour golf practice sessions a day."

That decided it. "Sir, I'm in!"

Review of meditation session:

- Awareness is everywhere. It's not just yours.

MONTH FIVE

DAY ONE OF RETREAT

I met the monk Tashi at the monastery as the sun was rising and we walked the 300 or so yards to the meditation cabin hidden in the woods on the other side. The view was stunning: a wide valley with enormous mountains on the other side.

The cabin was small but comfortable. "Tashi, I don't see a bed," I said nervously.

"The three-year retreatants sleep on their meditation cushions, sitting up," he answered soberly.

He then burst into laughter at my look of horror. "Rinpoche asked me to say that to get a reaction from you. You have permission to lie down. There is a futon in the cupboard."

"The shrine is set up in the traditional way, with candles and a small bowl of rice to hold the incense, which you should use every session. A monk will bring food three times a day and slide it into this small compartment in the back of the hut. You won't see him or anybody else, for that matter. You will hear the door sliding open three times a day."

I could only think of Pavlov's dog, salivating at the sound! We bowed to each other and my first retreat began.

I looked around nervously at the small, humble cabin. I realized I would be alone with my mind for a week. But the thought of hitting balls every day made me happy and brought up memories of my early cemetery practice range.

Going from one hour of meditation a day to six hours was quite an adjustment. For that first long session I may as well have been laying on a couch watching TV with a remote in my hand. The entire session was in the future.

I was worried. Can I do this? Would Rinpoche think I'm a failure if I leave with my tail between my legs? My mind was out of control.

And then came acceptance. I labeled that whole first hour 'thinking' and went back to the breath. I made a commitment to myself to stick it out, no matter what. From that came a little relaxation, and then I went back to the breathing. The last half hour was spent just doing the practice.

I timed my sessions with the length of time it took the incense to burn down. I heard the small door slide just as I was finishing – perfect timing. I rang the small gong to indicate the end of a session and went on to enjoy a simple but delicious Indian meal of vegetable curry and rice. I was grateful it wasn't that Bhutanese favourite dish of incredibly hot peppers and cheese!

Hitting balls

The yaks were on the far side of my private range and they had done a great job of mowing. After lunch I started my first golf practice session, starting small with a pitching wedge, just feeling the club in my hands. There were some bales of hay set out at different distances. I realized later that Rinpoche must have had them set out for me.

As rustic as it was, I couldn't have designed a more functional range. Well mown, lots of targets and some uneven lies - some rough and some with bare dirt. For years I've taught the value of random practice – creating as many different situations as you can. The only thing this range was missing was a putting green.

But my first practice session was blissful, taking me back to my cemetery driving range days. It was pure fun.

Meditation session

Tashi had given me a small booklet, translated into English, to inspire me: *The 10 Stages in the Development of Shamatha.*

I read the first few:

1) Directed attention: One develops the ability to focus on a chosen object (*Check, I thought to myself.*)

2) Continuous Attention: One can maintain continuous attention on the object for up to a minute (*On a good day, check.*)

3) Resurgent attention: One recovers swiftly when distracted from the object (*Sometimes, I thought.*)

4) Close Attention: The object of attention is no longer completely forgotten. (*Not so good on this one.*)

5) Tamed Attention: One takes satisfaction in *Samadhi*, or single-pointed concentration. (*Occasionally.*)

6) Pacified Attention: There is no longer resistance to attentional training. (*I think I'll skip this one.*)

10) Shamatha: One can effortlessly maintain concentration on an object for at least four hours; this is accompanied by greatly increased mental and physical pliancy and other positive side effects. (*I've got work to do.*)

I headed back to the meditation cushion. Intensive practice is just that – intense. But as soon as I realized there was no escape, I settled in.

Boring!

I couldn't wait for the next meal or the next range session. Nearly every thought I had was into the future, just trying to escape the tediousness. At least I stopped the tournament victory fantasies, which felt like a step in the right direction.

Then I was attacked by a hummer! That's the term that popped into my head after the third session of the day was spent with a song in my head. I think very highly of Bobby McFerrin as a performer. In fact, he's incredible. But try getting 'Don't Worry, Be Happy' stuck in your head for an hour and a half.

The painful part of this was that I was able to immediately notice when it clawed its way into my conscious mind. Therefore, I probably labeled it 'thinking' and went back to the breath at least 1,000 times. I guess that was an improvement over not noticing at all and blissfully zoning out on Bobby mindlessly. Maybe I am getting somewhere, I thought.

After the last session I fell asleep the minute my head hit the pillow. There was a fleeting moment of guilt that I wasn't sleeping sitting up, but it didn't last long.

DAY TWO OF RETREAT

The morning sit was uneventful, but painful. My legs hurt terribly. Determined to do the practice properly, I refrained from moving as long as possible.

I didn't run from the pain or try to change it; instead, I felt it fully, as my young teacher had suggested.

A strange thing happened. For a moment the pain was no longer mine. The deeper I felt it, the less I identified with it as something to avoid. I followed the throbbing rhythm, the different layers within the pain. I found it had a center and a periphery and it moved around.

The pain was 100% there, but it became an object to observe, not something to avoid. It was still pain, but it didn't hurt in the normal sense. I thought "I must be having a breakthrough; my meditation is working!" And immediately after having that thought, the pain came back in the normal sense!

Another issue that arose was keeping track of time. I would start a session at say 9, and at 9:10 I was already looking at how far the incense had burned and then look at my watch. Again at 9:18, and so on for an hour and a half.

I realized that this was seriously distracting, so I added some technology. My Casio watch had an alarm. I would set it at the beginning of a session for 40 minutes. I'd then do a few laps of walking meditation around the cabin and then sit another 40 minutes. I figured out that, by pacing myself, it took 10 minutes to circumambulate the cabin.

That filled up the entire session.

Hitting balls

I wanted to experiment with things I was learning on the cushion, such as feeling my body in a new way. I hit 7-irons with the intent of feeling my swing fully: the movement of pressure into the ground, the feeling of the club in my hands, the rhythm, the level of tension or relaxation in my body and where my mind was during the shot. In other words – the whole enchilada.

In a weird way the swing was no longer my swing, but in letting go of ownership I was able to feel it at a much deeper

"You can change your posture and rearrange yourself."

"There's no point in punishing yourself and trying to strain constantly."

"If you sit up properly, you are there. Your breathing follows naturally."

—Chögyam Trungpa Rinpoche
Dathun Letter

level. I wasn't trying to do anything. I was just being there watching a swing.

I hadn't felt that since I was a kid. It was liberating.

Afternoon meditation session

A few minutes into the session, I discovered my head. I should say I felt it balanced on top of my spine. Any subtle movements I made, forward or sideways, and I was out of balance.

When I went out of balance, I felt tension to have to hold my head up. When I could find that fine balance, my shoulders relaxed and my head hung naturally. Once I found the balance, my focus improved. I could look directly at the ball.

I flashed on the golf posture and how one's head, weighing 10 or 11 pounds, can really ruin a shot if it's in the wrong place. Fortunately, I labeled that whole conversation 'thinking' before I spun out too much.

Then it occurred to me that I was just going through the motions. My breathing was forced, not natural. I was trying to meditate, rather than just meditating. I labeled this 'dull mind', and remembered the antidote: faith in the practice.

As always, just by noticing this dullness directly rather than ignoring it softened the edges. My breathing became natural as I allowed the practice to settle.

DAY THREE OF RETREAT

I was doing my morning sitting practice, looking out a window due east, before sunrise. The sun was coming up behind the mountain in front of me and the sky was vast and clear.

A solitary bird flew across my field of vision and out again. It reminded me of my thoughts: When I didn't hold on to them, they simply passed through, leaving no record or trail. I was feeling pretty good about my meditation at this point, but that too was a thought. My train of thought was now

> "When I play my best golf, I feel as if I'm in a fog, standing back watching the earth in orbit with a golf club in my hands."
> —Hall of Fame LPGA Golfer Mickey Wright

> "Awareness per se is curative."
> —Psychiatrist Fritz Perls

subtle… *Wow, my mind is like that sky, and the bird flew through without my mind being distracted.*

What a great meditator I am!

Then I heard the sound of buzzing and I noticed a small fly in the window I was looking out of. Unlike the bird, this little bug did grab my attention and completely seized my mind for a while. I got a little angry that such a small thing could commandeer my mind, when suddenly the blazing sun rose from behind the mountain.

Any thoughts of the bug completely disappeared and my mind stopped as I witnessed this incredible event.

Afterward, the whole analogy became clear to me: sometimes the little, seemingly inconsequential thoughts, being so close, are the hardest to let go of. But if you can keep attentive to the big picture in front of you, i.e., the whole enchilada, then the small thoughts become just that – small thoughts that "vanish into emptiness like the imprint of a bird in the sky," a quote Rinpoche's teacher used.

After that my practice really settled. The few thoughts that came were mostly of gratitude for the gift Rinpoche gave me. I vowed to do a retreat every year of my life.

Later during the same session, I heard the gong from the monastery in the distance. Oddly, the sound wasn't separate from me; it felt like it was inside of me, a part of me.

A thought rose: *My pain is no longer mine, yet a sound 300 yards away is part of me.* I had no choice but to label it 'thinking' and go back to the breath.

Between sessions I found myself talking out loud to myself. It was the longest time I have ever spent totally alone. I resolved that this wasn't really a problem, as I wasn't talking back to myself!

Golf session

On the practice tee, I was starting to notice my mind and body at a new level. Standing before the shot I did a short meditation: checking first feelings and thoughts that arose, then my body, and then the other senses – sight, sound, smell. I saved taste for dinnertime.

Sometimes before the shot I noticed that I was trying to do something. Other times I came to the shot from a pure love of ball-striking. I remembered Rinpoche saying we are human *beings*, not human *do-ings*. The shots that came from *doing* felt a little stiffer, or more wooden. Those that flowed from *being* were freer and more powerful. I made a mental note to bring this up to Rinpoche and get his feedback.

Meditation session

Back on the meditation cushion, I noticed I had recurring thoughts and that each one was accompanied by a specific feeling. I tried the method of viewing these as somebody else's thoughts and feelings, which worked for a while. Then I had an image that these thoughts and feelings were just flying through space, hitting people randomly. They weren't mine, just like the neutrinos that are constantly passing through our bodies are not ours (or are they?).

That worked for a while as well. But then I had an image of mountains that would rise and fall in an instant in my mind. These mountains were under the ocean. If they grew high enough, they would break through the surface of the ocean to the light of day – or to my conscious mind. Each mountain had an associated feeling which was at the base of the mountain, propping it up. For example, anger was molten rock.

The mountains that broke through were the thoughts in my mind at that moment. And there were lots of other mountains clamouring to burst into my consciousness when the current one fell away.

Each mountain each had its own storyline too, and a feeling that went with it. And they were pretty much the same every time.

There was the "What I'm going to do when I get home?" mountain, a "Is this just a waste of time?" mountain, etc. If I was attracted to a mountaintop that popped up, I might go over to it in my little row boat and climb on. As soon as I did, a string of mountains, a whole range would present

"An increasingly common answer within the field of psychology, especially evolutionary psychology, is that the mind is 'modular.' In this view, your mind is composed of lots of specialized modules."
—Robert Wright
Why Buddhism Is True

"No thought,
No reflection,
No analysis,
No cultivation,
No intention,
Let it settle itself"
—The six precepts of Tilopa

127

itself. This was the train of thoughts that grew because I got attached to one thought.

If I was able to pat the mountain on its head and row on, it would quickly disappear. Touch and go.

That worked for a while as well, meaning I was able to disassociate from the thought while still being aware of it. A song entered my mind:

Row, row, row your boat,
gently down the stream.
Merrily, merrily, merrily,
life is but a dream.

"Maybe life was a dream," I thought. Rinpoche had said so on numerous occasions.

Or maybe this was like a swing thought that works wonders one day, but not the next. I'd have to wait and see.

DAY FOUR OF RETREAT

The fourth morning was cold. During my first meditation session I laughed out loud, as I could actually see a cloud of vapor go out during my exhale. I was really being the breath.

I had settled into a routine: Practice meditation, practice golf, eat. Practice meditation, practice golf, eat. Practice meditation, eat. Practice meditation, sleep.

The practice was even infiltrating my meals. For most of my life I would wolf down a meal in record time. On retreat I slowed that down. The subtle flavors of the curries, the sizzle of an occasional hot pepper, the texture of the rice – these became objects of mindfulness. And the more aware I was of the subtleties of each meal, the slower I would eat and chew.

Unlike meals back home, the amounts were much less, but just right. I wasn't hungry after eating, just satisfied.

In the meditation practice, my relationship to boredom was beginning to change. I looked at boredom as I did with pain, noticing the subtleties. Why am I showing so much aversion? Why do I want so much to escape it?

As I accepted boredom and allowed it to be, the more it changed into clarity and an overwhelming feeling of peace. *Maybe I'm fooling myself, but could this be a glimpse of egolessness?*

Golf practice

On the range I easily brought this deeper clarity and acceptance to hitting balls. I saw bad shots in a new way. Previously, my first response would have been anger, then self-consciousness, then a search for excuses: somebody moved, I have a sore back, whatever.

Now, carrying non-judgemental awareness to a mistake created curiosity rather than a knee-jerk response. Was there tension before the shot? Was the tempo smooth? Was I approaching the ball from doing or being? Was my mind distracted? If so, where did it go? Were my senses engaged? Did I have the intention before the shot of where I wanted it to go?

And after that short moment of curiosity, did I go into the deadly 'fix it' mode, or was I able to use what I learned to notice, then to let go? Touch and go.

After my pre-practice stretching session, I took aim at the 50-yards-out bale. The direction and contact were very good, but my distance control was inconsistent: 10 yards over, five yards short – not good enough to make birdies.

This was not a technical swing deficiency, but more senses related – visual, feel. I did an experiment. Looking 90 degrees left from the target, I picked out a bush that appeared to be 50 yards out. Then I turned my back to the target and picked out a rock 50 yards away.

I drew a mental 50-yard circle with me at the center. Then an image of a big bubble appeared, with a 50-yard radius, spreading in all directions, with me at the center.

I looked up, visualizing a tree 40 yards high, giving me a 10 yard leeway to hit over it at 50 yards. Then I tried mentally to go down 50 yards into the ground. At this point I drew a blank. I was unable to go down into the ground; there was

"My feet don't lie to me."
—World champion blind golfer Brian McLeod, Truro, Nova Scotia, on reading greens.

129

a blockage. I was trying to make a full 50 yard globe in all directions, but failing in the downward dimension.

I sat down on a hay bale to contemplate this obstacle. I knew that humans have an electrical charge. And electricians are careful to establish a ground connection. Maybe the blockage was electrical in nature?

So I took my shoes off. It was a dry, pleasant day, so my feet felt liberated. I sat still on the bale, feeling my feet being connected to the ground. Following the outbreath, I directed my awareness down, through the soles of my feet, into the earth.

At first, I was only breaking the surface, going down a few inches. But with each outbreath I went deeper.

As I went down, I felt a connection to the earth like I have never felt before. I was getting energy; the soles of my feet were tingling, alive.

What started as an exercise in distance control evolved into something much more primordial. I flashed on the massive size of the globe and the unfathomable strength it held. Was there a way to tap into that power consciously?

After a while, after getting off the hay bale and standing up, going down 50 yards into the ground became easy. Once I did, I recreated the bubble 360 degrees around me. At that point distance control was no longer only visual – I could feel it in my feet.

For the remainder of the session I hit balls with my shoes off, feeling this connection. It was the most fun I've had in years. I ended the session throwing darts at the hay bale, hitting it more often than missing.

Meditation session

I found the image of underwater mountains rising into view and then falling away intriguing. Because these thought mountains carried their own feelings, I could feel them rising sometimes even before the thought fully formed. It was

"I was just hanging in there with my mind."
—Tiger Woods, after the last round of the 2018 PGA Championship, where on the front nine he missed every fairway, yet still remained near the lead.

like a bubble in my consciousness that never broke through, or pressure without puncture.

I gave myself permission to use tricks, such as the mountain image and the thoughts-are-from-the-person-next-to-me, as valid ways to view my thoughts non-judgementally without buying into them. It's the same as a swing thought: if it doesn't resonate, move on to one that works.

DAY FIVE OF RETREAT

That night I was in and out of lucid dreaming. Once I realised that flying, as fun as it was, wasn't furthering my path, I decided to practice golf.

In my dream state Gollum appeared in the gallery. This time, I invited him to talk with me on the green. I wanted to know how I could deal with this fear in an environment I could control.

> "I love playing golf. I love practicing. I love everything about it, I feel awfully fortunate."
> —Matt Kuchar

After driving the green again (it was a dream after all!), I was left with a 10-foot putt. Over crawled Gollum, who whispered in my ear: "You have the yips. You will always have the yips."

Instantly I was back at age 13. I was playing golf with my brother, but between shots we were running, being chased by Gollum. Suddenly I stopped and turned around to face him: "I no longer need to run from you. I am playing for one reason only, because I love the game."

Instantly, my metronome ally appeared. In my dream, the beat was close to waltz time: 1-2-1.

> "Golf is a privilege. You never 'have' to play golf, you 'get' to play golf."
> —Harvey Penick

Turning back to the ball I matched my stroke to the tempo and buried the eagle into the middle of the cup. I woke up then, feeling totally refreshed.

Laying in bed thinking about the dream, I realized that I had been playing golf for the wrong reasons. I love the game, that's enough reason to play. I moved beyond the old fear of missing by facing it.

I didn't know then, but I would never yip another putt

again. That's not to say I didn't miss, even from short range. But the fearful, awful twitch was gone forever.

Meditation session

I had been breaking up the meditation sessions with a short walking meditation around my little cabin. For the first four days I saw this as a chance to stretch my stiff legs. But on the fifth day that changed.

The walking session was evoking the same responses as my sitting practice. But the movement made it feel in some ways more relevant to being in the world with the mind of meditation. I began to expand the walking practice, not as an escape, but as another powerful way to practice mindfulness.

Heel, toe, stride, heel, toe, stride. When a thought arose, I went back to my feet. (The most recurring thought was: *I must try this on the course!*)

Golf practice

That day on the range I realized that my body felt different. I was stiffer from the long hours of sitting and felt a bit slower. Rather than trying to swing at my normal pace, I matched my swing to how my body felt. Surprisingly, I hit it further and most shots were right on the screws.

It was by far my best practice session yet.

Walking out to pick up balls afterward, I thought about how it was a shame more people didn't practice golf this way. There was a sense of walking meditation and contemplation while gathering balls. It brought back memories of my crooked-headstone range. Only then I usually had only two or three balls.

Usually people hit balls as fast as they can, without thinking. If they then had to pick them up, there would be such a different mindset.

The big lesson for me this day, was, as golfing great Sam Snead said: "Dance with the one that brung ya."

"At the most basic level, physical awareness relates to the state or condition of your body at a given moment."
—Nilsson and Marriott
Be a Player

If your body feels slow or sluggish, don't try to play the same as you would when you feel energized and dynamic.

Meditation session

I was getting better at noticing the feelings beneath the underwater mountains before they formed into thoughts. I started to label these feelings 'anger', 'fear', 'dullness' and so on, rather than just saying 'thinking' when a thought arose.

I was still catching myself future-planning, trying to cover up my impatience and boredom...and there was the mindless humming or song lyrics. It took a while to identify the underlying feeling there, but finally something resonated. It was my imaginary inner mini-me CEO saying "What about me?" And beneath that was the fear of groundlessness or non-existence. The built-in need to pass along DNA is incredibly strong; without a self, how can the species survive? It turns out, much better. Look at the world today, how has self-importance worked for us?

The past was another mountain that would sometimes pop up. I was in a horrible car accident five years earlier, while driving at night in a rainstorm. Miraculously, nobody was hurt. But there was a moment that felt like minutes – where the car was flying sideways through the air at 70 miles an hour. That was real groundlessness, not knowing where or how it would land. I don't remember feeling afraid, though. I was more curious. Whatever was going to happen was going to happen.

The car ended up landing on its side on a snowbank. We climbed out, straight up through the passenger door. There were many ways that my companions and I could have been killed: hitting a tree or another car, or landing where there was no snow. As it was, the car was nearly bent into an L.

I had to have therapy around that accident because of a developing fear of driving in the rain at night.

> "The bad news is that you are falling through the air, nothing to hang onto, no parachute. The good news is that there is no ground."
> —Chögyam Trungpa Rinpoche

DAY SIX OF RETREAT

Meditation session

Carrying over from the golf session yesterday, I felt very attuned to my body and senses. I also felt much more energized and made a mental note of how that would affect my golf shots during range practice.

The meditation in the first session felt distracted, so I went back to the gazing exercise Rinpoche taught me. There is a difference between looking and seeing. It wasn't about what I was looking at, but how.

My eyes were bouncing around, probably because my mind was bouncing around. As soon as I noticed that and allowed my gaze to quiet, a vast mental quiet came over me. The only thought that temporarily pulled me away was that I needed to try this on the range.

It dawned on me that the term 'focus' can mean clear vision as well as mental concentration. It was not a staring or forced quiet, which is an oxymoron.

I remembered Rinpoche saying many times, in many ways: "The moment you notice you are gone, you are already back." It's all about the noticing.

Range practice

After a delicious lunch and some stretching, I brought my clubs out to the range. Picking a bale about 160 yards out, I took out the 7-iron.

The energized feeling in my body remained and I remembered how that state disrupted focus in meditation. So when I stood behind the ball, I just looked out. Not visualizing, not planning, just looking with quiet eyes.

The intention to hit the bale was there, but I wasn't trying to hit the bale, I was just looking quietly. What happened next I could only describe as 'trust'.

I had the intention to hit the target. I had an unforced

> "When I see, I see what I see. When I don't see, what I see is me."
> —Unknown

view of what was in my field of vision. I exerted no conscious effort to hit the target. Miraculously, that cocktail produced a feeling of groundlessness and the shot came off perfectly, landing just over the hay bale.

As I assessed the shot afterward, the only conclusion I could come to was that I had hit it without trying or particularly caring. That led me to a deeper level of inquiry. If I didn't try or care, what was it that made that shot? I could only think it was my subconscious, the part of me working behind the scenes on so much that I do, from driving a car to breathing, to keeping my heart beating – a part of me that's hidden from my ordinary mind. I made a note to ask Rinpoche about the Buddhist view of the subconscious.

The shot was so exhilarating that I didn't even try another. I added a fifth meditation session instead.

DAY SEVEN OF RETREAT

I woke up feeling sad that this was my last day of retreat. But I also felt a sense of faith – faith that the meditation and teachings I was receiving on how the mind works were for real and good for me.

The day was uneventful but beautiful. Both the sadness and faith permeated everything I did. I renewed my vow to do a retreat every year of my life.

For the last few hours of my incredible week I packed up my few belongings, cleaned my tiny cabin and went to bed early.

Meditation session – debrief

The day after ending my retreat, I had a short meeting with Rinpoche to debrief. The colors of the trees seemed brighter on my walk up to the monastery. The chattering of the monkeys in those trees was delightfully playful. I felt lighter and couldn't stop smiling.

"Well done, Ed," Rinpoche said by way of greeting.

Recent studies have shown that visualizing right before we perform actually hurts performance. The studies found the most useful place to use visualization was away from competition.

This study was published in *The Sports Psychologist*, March 2016. —Mike Hebron Golf Science Lab.com

---

"I seem to be a verb." —Buckminister Fuller

"You stuck it out. Anything to report, any questions?"

"Sir, it was special," I replied. "Thank you for allowing me the place to do it and for motivating me. You are so right – my practice deepened. And I feel that my golf game has changed too."

"How so? What did you learn?"

"Many things," I began. "I experienced the emptiness of my swing. For fleeting moments, I experienced it objectively, almost as if it weren't mine. It felt like a verb, not a noun."

"And I found the difference between doing a shot and hitting a shot from a place of being. I tuned into my body and mind before hitting and realized that my swing changes minutely depending on where my mind and body are."

I continued. "I discovered a new way to deal with bad shots, by being curious rather than reacting with anger or disgust. It feels like I can learn something from bad shots."

"Finally, I had the experience of action without trying, or even caring. Somehow my subconscious mind took over, like I was on autopilot."

I was ready to ask the question that was left lingering from my experience on the retreat. "My big question is: what is the subconscious mind?"

He seemed very happy with the question.

His eyes lit up: "In my lineage, it is taught that there are nine kinds of consciousness," he explained. "The first six can be accessed with your ordinary mind. The last three could be called 'the subconscious.'"

"The first six are the five senses and the mind you are working with in your meditation every day."

"The seventh is that huge self that you glimpsed, the one you described like sticky flypaper. It is also the consciousness that judges what is good and what is not, the place where grasping, feelings and most dreams reside."

"The eighth consciousness is called *alaya* mind. It is what psychologists would call the 'unconscious mind.' It is also called 'storehouse consciousness' and goes on after your body dies. At some point you might study karma; knowledge you don't need right now to further your understanding."

"The ninth is the level of pure consciousness, the clear light consciousness. This is at the basis of all of existence – primordial purity."

"Back to golf," he said, and we both laughed heartily, "the consciousness that you are asking about is the seventh and eighth. For our work, you could lump them together as your subconscious. *Ca va?*"

"Works for me. See you at the range."

Golf session, showing Rinpoche what I learned

The yaks didn't seem to want to move that day, so we walked the length of the field to the private range that I called home for that unforgettable week of retreat.

"Ed, teach me what you learned," Rinpoche said.

I was far from being able to present these discoveries to students. I'd have to dig deep to rediscover what they were; at that point just brief epiphanies.

"OK," I said taking a breath, "Here goes: The big picture is that just being there and allowing the swing to form because of the situation gave better results than trying to force the ball to a target. When I was able to do that, my swing was ever-changing, to fit the shot. Trying to implant an unchanging swing to different situations created chaos."

He stepped over with a hybrid in his hands. "Show me how to do that," he asked.

Oh boy, I thought. *This is one of those no-escape moments.*

"Rinpoche, for me to tell you about the mental game is like showing Picasso how to draw. I feel embarrassed."

He just stood there, waiting.

"OK," I said, giving in. "Let's say you want to go toward the last bale on the left, around 200 yards out. First, think to yourself or say out loud: 'That's where I want the ball to go.' Make it the starting point of the shot. Then, notice how your body feels and if there are any feelings that come up. This step might change the intended target."

I continued. "On the course you would look at many factors to determine the shot in advance: lie, wind, how you feel, etc. Here, the lie is good with no unusual conditions."

"From all this you will pick a club." He still had the hybrid in his hands so I continued. "Now just stand behind the ball and look out. My epiphany was that I didn't say 'visualize it', but just look."

As the words came out of my mouth, I remembered the way I was looking. My eyes rested on the target, but my vision was taking in the area right, left, above and below it.

"Let your eyes rest on the target, without anything added," I said. If I had been teaching somebody back home, I might have added: "your subconscious will take care of the rest. Trust it."

Rinpoche stepped up to the ball and hit a weak pull. As the first shot of the day, without any warm up, it was to be expected.

"Sir, another discovery was that I could short-circuit anger, embarrassment or excuse-making by using the meditative method of just noticing," I explained. Then the word 'curiosity' came up.

"The questions I asked myself were: Am I tense? Does my tempo seem athletic? Am I trying to force the ball somewhere? Am I distracted? The bottom line is not to try to fix anything on the next swing. Just like you can't fix a thought or feeling, just noticing is the most powerful response."

"Ed, that was the first ball I have hit in two weeks, outside of a dream," Rinpoche said. "It takes my body a few swings to get the flow."

I knew that wasn't an excuse or him protecting his ego. It was a fact.

"What else did you come up with?" he asked.

"Sir, I discovered an obvious fact: that my body and mind are different every day. If I felt slow and sluggish and was able to notice that, I matched my swing to that feeling. If I was excited and energetic, I needed to harness that. And I found resting my eyes on the ball an effective antidote to a speedy mind and body."

"You mentioned yesterday of having a feeling that your swing didn't exist. Can you teach that to me?" His eyes were laughing, but the rest of his expression was inscrutable.

I knew he wouldn't let me off the hook, so I decided to 'fake it 'til I made it'.

"You've taught me that in Buddhism there is emptiness and no-self. Lumping them together, they mean action may be occurring, yet there is no CEO directing it. The action grows from the situation at hand."

"It's no different in golf," I continued. "As I said earlier, the swing in many ways doesn't exist until there is a target and the conditions that exist at that moment. A golf swing is a verb, not a noun. The best way to experience the swing as being 'empty' is to meditate."

Rinpoche stood very still and I felt like I could see the entire universe in his eyes. Was I looking at the ninth consciousness?

"Well done, Ed," he finally said. "Next week in our meditation session I would like to introduce the term 'dependent arising.'"

I couldn't believe my good fortune to be learning about my mind in this way, with golf as the common ground.

Review of golf session:

• Taking what I had learned and teaching it to others.

Dream – the dragon

That night my intention to lucid dream was supercharged: I would explore egolessness. Soon after dropping off, I jumped – and flew – quickly into a dream. It was in the form of a story that was unfolding as I watched. It was spoken in a deep, calming voice that didn't seem to have any place of origin.

Many, many years ago, dragons walked on and flew above this earth. They were known in the Bhutanese culture as inscrutable, in others as powerful, rich and just. As long as people were respectful, the dragons left them alone.

But as time went on, man began to encroach on the dragon's lairs and even tried to destroy them. The dragons seemed to disappear and people stopped talking about them as before. They became part of the stories of old, like the unicorns and gnomes.

However, they did not vanish. They only disappeared from our eyes, waiting for the proper time to come out again and command the respect that they deserve. You see, one of the tricks that dragons use is to become part of the earth. They blend in perfectly, just waiting. And dragons can wait a very long time.

In recent days, the dragons have taken to blending into golf courses. The size and shape are perfect, the land is nicely cleared and the humans found walking there offer a soothing massage.

The story begins when a young dragon, known as Gom, began to feel restless. He blended with the Thimpu course, on which he

"The light of the clear light mind does not refer to physical light. It refers to the capacity of mind to perceive its contents, and to know."
—Andrew Holecek

"If the mind and body are connected and the earth and body have a connection, then the earth and your mind have a connection."

"So play golf with the intention of being connected to the course, the land."
—Katie Hanczaryk

fit perfectly. On the surface all was well, except he craved more, he wanted expression – he wanted to play. He saw and felt all the golfers every day on his muscular body and decided to try golf himself. But he couldn't, without help.

The problem was that playing himself was a bit like looking into his own eyes: impossible without a mirror. The mirror he needed was a human who would give up his body for a few hours so that Gom could use it and enjoy some creative time. You see, another gift of dragons is transference of consciousness. But the right person had to be found.

In this dream/story that person was me. Being a lucid dream, I decided to take an active role. I was no longer being told a story – suddenly I was part of the story.

I decided to open up completely and let the dragon take over my consciousness.

The dragon was ready and in an instant the mind transference was complete. The dragon's mind entered my body. Gom was playing himself. Understand, there was still enough of me left to use those years of experience to read greens, select clubs and so on, and I still enjoyed chatting with his playing partners. But for all intents and purposes, I was just an agent, a mirror.

And as far as Gom was concerned, it would be no fun to have a hole-in-one every time, nor would that be possible with the wind and other conditions out of his control. As well, I was human and my body and mind changed from day to day.

But what a liberating experience! Gom played a round with some weird bounces (and lucky breaks) and in the dream I swung more freely than I had since playing as a kid. The resulting best score ever was not even the point; on the next shot the dragon may decide to go into the woods to make it interesting!

I woke up abruptly, with an understanding of action without self. I knew that these bursts of enlightenment usually didn't stick around. It dawned on me that enlightenment with a capital E might be just that: moment to moment. It's not

"Most people, when they have their first lucid dream, notice some anomaly, some odd object or event in their dream that catalyzes the awareness that they are dreaming."
—B. Alan Wallace
Dreaming Yourself Awake

like getting a diploma and you're good for life. I needed to ask Rinpoche to clarify.

The next time out on the course, I made a mental note to not 'play the course', but rather to 'play with' the golf course.

Meditation session – dependent arising

When I met Rinpoche at the monastery, he looked like himself again. But the look he had given me the other day, like the entire universe was behind his eyes, haunted me.

We sat for 10 minutes. Since my retreat I had been able to stay present for much longer and watch what was going on in my mind and body much sooner.

When the sound of the gong subsided, Rinpoche spoke: "The Buddha, after many years of searching, decided to stop and sit still. He sat under a Bodhi tree and vowed to stay until he discovered the truth."

"Up to that point, he understood everything I have taught you thus far. But still he was not fully enlightened. The final understanding was what I would like to talk to you about today: dependent arising, or *paticca samuppada*."

"It has been described as two sheaves of wheat leaning up against each other. One is standing only because the other is standing. The layman's description would be cause and effect."

"Your senses interact with the world and when they do, feelings arise. You have experienced that in your meditation practice. When feelings arise, so arises wanting to either bring the object of your senses toward you, to push it away, or to ignore it."

"Dependent arising is the way things work; interdependent, arising simultaneously, moment to moment. Doing and doer, knowing and knower, perceiver and perceived, mind and matter – all are part of a network, a web."

Regarding the Universe: "Do you do it, or does it do you?" —Alan Watts

"Leave the seeing in the seeing, leave the hearing in the hearing, leave the thinking in the thinking." —Khyentse Rinpoche

"This is where the rubber meets the road," Rinpoche said, and I could tell that he was proud of this phrase. "When feeling becomes craving. At that point you can cut the negative cycle and introduce an enlightened experience. If you can let the feeling arise without reacting to it, the unhappy spiral is broken."

"As a student of Darwinian evolution at Oxford, I have learned that survival and passing along our DNA is hardwired to be our purpose in life. We have developed feelings to keep the species going. We react to those feelings to stay alive and pass on our lineage. The practice you are doing can be called conscious evolution. You are changing your brain and directing your mind toward basic goodness."

"Keep practicing," he said in conclusion. "Let's meet at the golf course next time."

"Thank you, Rinpoche."

> ### Review of Meditation Session:
>
> - *Paticca samuppada* – dependent arising. The sense of *you* and the object of your senses arising simultaneously. There is no *you* until a sense interacts with a sense object. There is no golf swing until there is a situation that creates it.

Golf session – gathering and releasing energy

I came upon Rinpoche practicing on the range. His address position seemed off.

During the time I was in Bhutan, white belts were all the rage for golfers. No teaching pro would be caught dead without one. Without my usual assessment equipment handy, I used my belt, asking Rinpoche to put it on. It was way too big but it would work for our purposes.

I wanted to see if his hips were tilted from front to back,

"Buddhism is an evolutionary sport."
—Robert Thurman

"The education of attention would be an education par excellence."
—William James

higher in the back. Most people have a 10-degree tilt, viewed from the side. His belt was level. This probably meant that his weight was on his heels and his back was too rounded.

I told him to set up to hit a shot but to hold that stance. I walked around to his front and with one finger pushed on his chest. He fell backward.

"You want your hips in a natural slightly-up-in-the-back position," I said. "If you know I am going to push you, how would you stand?"

He naturally got balanced and grounded.

"OK," I said. "Let's go play a few holes."

On the first tee, Rinpoche took the pose I saw him in before: pointing the grip end of the club upward at a 45-degree angle toward the target, standing sideways to the target line, his right arm pointing down 45 degrees.

He turned to me and said: "There is nobody behind us, I think this is a good time to discuss Kyudo Zen archery and how it could apply to golf."

"The essence of this tradition is to gather energy to the heart, then releasing that energy with focus and precision. As you glimpsed on retreat, there is no attachment to the result. When I do this, the energy of the environment is also being invited."

"Many *tulkus* are known to be able to change the weather and create wind."

As he talked, a tiny whirlwind formed in front of us. Seeing that stopped my mind.

"This is not a magic trick," he said, reading my mind, "it is just being in tune with the phenomenal world around you."

I wondered why it never rained on our lessons, even on days when it was forecast.

He continued: "In Tibetan Buddhism there are many hand movements and body postures that evoke resonance in the body. I have come up with this as a *mudra*, combining golf with Kyudo. Try it."

A tulku is a reincarnate custodian of a specific lineage of teachings in Tibetan Buddhism who is given empowerments and trained from a young age by students of his or her predecessor.
—Wikipedia

143

I assumed the posture I'd seen him do: standing sideways, toes pointing at the target line, arms stretched out.

"Now look up, where the club is pointing," he instructed. "Feel the energy gathering in the area of your heart. Now with a sharp shout, send the energy out into space."

My shout was very weak, wimpy. He howled with laughter.

"Watch me."

His pose was elegant but he still had the powerful look of a Samurai warrior. For many moments he stood still and I swear I could feel electricity forming.

"PHAT!" he shouted so loudly that I jumped.

"The release of sound is critical in the release of the bow," he explained. "It is letting go of the arrow and the result of the shot."

I thought of high-level tennis players making loud sounds as they hit the ball. Somehow I didn't see this happening in golf, but the gathering of energy was a keeper.

"You have a lot of new protocols from your retreat," he said. "This one is for me, having studied Kyudo intensively. For you, maybe fit in the gathering of energy to the heart, during the initial intent phase of your routine."

"Sir, I'm just being honest...there's no way I'm going to do that back home!"

We both had a good laugh.

"But I do have a question," I said. "Would you recommend doing walking meditation between shots?"

"No," he said, to my surprise. "Remember the *dralas*? Enjoy the beauty of the course, the wind in the trees, the soft ground, enjoy your playing partners. Once you near the ball, then you could ease into more of a practice mind."

Top golfer Greg Norman, carried a book in his golf bag *Zen in the Martial Arts*, by Joe Hyams. The book describes a Japanese term *Mushin*, which means no mind. Zen is a Japanese tradition based on the practice of sitting meditation.

> **Review of Golf Lesson:**
>
> - In the Kyudo Zen archery tradition, energy is gathered in the heart, then explosively released.

The final chapter

We bowed, sat for 10 minutes and continued sitting after the sound of the gong was long gone. This was to be the last time I would ever see my beloved teacher in this form, as my assignment had come to an end. "Rinpoche, how will I be able to continue learning back home without your help?", I asked. He straightened his robes and looked at me directly. "Ed, my work with you has been pointing out. If I point at the moon, don't focus on the finger, focus on the moon."

"You have Buddha nature, your mind is the Buddha. The path you are on is to realize that. The Buddha is in your golf swing. You have all the tools you need to continue. Keep up your meditation practice and the path will continue to open up before you."

"Ed, now it is time for you to tell the story exactly like it happened."

"Yes, Sir. Thank you, Rinpoche, for your brilliant teaching. I love you."

What really happened

I wish I could say that I went on to win a big tournament, or that he finally broke 80. Or even better, that I became fully enlightened, but that wouldn't be true.

Most of this story was true. I did teach the juniors in Bhutan for four months, including at a remote monastery. I did have the yips, which were healed. I did invent Golchery. I did have a relationship with golf which was an escape. When I realized that and learned to love the game, my yips were cured.

The teachings from the monk were really a culmination of many teachers in the Tibetan Buddhist, Shambhala and Zen traditions. My root teacher was Trungpa Rinpoche.

The golf lessons with the young Rinpoche were distilled from the tens of thousands of golfers I have taught through the years. The only thing they were missing was dream yoga and an intimate understanding of the mind.

Trungpa Rinpoche at The Regent's Open, late 1970s.
Photo: Robert Del Tredici, from his book *Trungpa Photographs.*

Most of the details about my early life and all the Bhutan stories are true, except for the time with Rinpoche and the retreat. I have, however, done many solitary retreats in Cape Breton, Nova Scotia, Vermont and Colorado. Instead of teaching in Maryland as in the story, I turned professional in Boulder at Lake Valley Country Club, later moving to Jacksonville where my southern belle was from. Instead of Columbia Country Club, the famous course where I worked was Sawgrass.

I did take lessons from Bill Strausbaugh at Colombia Country Club in Maryland. It was during one lesson that I realized I wanted to be a teaching pro, to be like him.

As I wrote, the young monk took on a life of his own. The things he taught me I actually learned from many teachers. Some information came from books. It all came back to me through him.

The young monk became sort of a healer for me. Through him, and not really knowing what would happen next, my practice really did deepen.

I met Trungpa Rinpoche in Boulder, Colorado in 1974, and studied with him until he died in 1986. Trungpa was one of the most influential Tibetan teachers to teach in North America.

By 1981 I had done six one-month group retreats (10 hours a day of meditation) and numerous solitary retreats.

My wife Donna and I moved to Jacksonville in 1980, where I worked at Sawgrass and other clubs. In 1991 we moved to Nova Scotia to be near the large *sangha* there.

I had the good fortune while in Jacksonville to have befriended a gifted teacher, Norrie Wright. He had golf in his DNA, having learned from his grandfather, a professional who came from Scotland and was one of the founding members of the PGA. He passed his knowledge along to Norrie, who then passed it on to me.

There were many golfers in the Buddhist sangha, all students of Trungpa. One of the golfers in those days was Barry Boyce. Barry is editor-in-chief of *Mindful Magazine* and very connected to many people on the path of meditation throughout the world.

Aside from being one of the most enjoyable chaps to play golf with, Barry has a creative mind. His initials are BB, so he gave each golfer in the mix a 'B' name. His own name was 'Blather'. Others were Babe, Bunker (miss you Nan), Belle, Birdie, Bellow (Captain Forbes, who once during every round would yell something at the top of his lungs, usually profane), Blast, Bliss, Bland, Blend, Backswing, Blessed and Bleak, Bow, Belligerent and too many others to name. Broast was the only person to petition for a name change; he became 'Better'.

For some reason I was the only golfer whose name didn't start with B. I became Prince Edward, referencing the beautiful island province next to Nova Scotia – Prince Edward Island.

Just before leaving Boulder, I had the good fortune to drive Trungpa Rinpoche around Lake Valley Golf Course in a golf car. He was not feeling well so I got a call from Marty Janowicz, one of his close attendants, asking if he could come out. I got to be his driver, as I knew the course.

He loved the gentle moguls on the dog-leg seventh hole, asking me to go back and come down the fairway many times. Going up hole number eight, he pointed at a tree and asked me to park underneath. We were facing east, away from the mountains.

He pointed out that this was actually two trees that had grown together, something I had never noticed in 100 rounds at the course. As we looked out, he mentioned that this was a power spot in the whole valley. I always did love hole number eight, but for different reasons.

We sat in silence for a while, looking east. Finally, I cranked up the courage to ask a question: "Rinpoche, Donna and I are moving to Florida. I am a golf professional and a teacher. Do you have any advice for me?"

He thought for a very long time, then answered in his very high voice: "It's OK, as long as you teach awareness".

I spent the next 37 years trying to understand what that meant and how to do it. In 1992, to help me remember, I named my teaching business Awareness Golf.

Many years later, Donna and I went to Boulder to visit old friends. I took her out on a golf car to the tree on hole eight, which was still there. We sat, facing east, when a soft blanket of white began to fall on us from the tree. It was a cottonwood tree, picking that moment to shed some flowers. To me it was my root guru saying hello.

This book was a joy to write. I had none of the writer angst and anguish that I heard writers go through during the process. That was because on every page the young Rinpoche came alive. I never knew what he was going to say, until it was on paper. Most of this was written on retreat in Nova Scotia, in a little cabin next to a field. I hit balls and meditated every day.

In the end, when I look back at all the powerful, spiritual, wonderful people that I have met and that magical land, what I remember best are the kids.

And FYI, I did see a Tulku create a whirlwind.

APPENDIX 1

GOLCHERY RULES

- The buh should be set at a distance apart of 15 yards, for the standard game. Newer golfers should have the buh set at closer range.
- There is a standard buh issued by the Bhutan Youth Golf Association. If this is not available, the buh can be made from cardboard.

Golchery Format

- Teams are chosen, each team chooses a name. Player number 1, 2, 3, 4, etc are determined by the captain. This order must be kept the entire game.
- The captains are responsible for keeping score.
- Both teams start on the same side. Player 1 on team A hits one putt. Player 1 on team B then hits one putt. Player 1 on team A then hits a second putt. Player 1 on team B then hits a second putt. Then both players walk to the other side to retrieve balls (and cheer for their team).
- The same process is repeated for player 2, 3, 4, up to the last player. If there is an uneven number on the teams, one player will hit twice on the team with the fewest members. The player hitting twice must change each round, allowing each member a chance to hit twice.
- Once all players have hit, the same process is repeated from the other side. This is repeated until one team reaches the target score in the fast game, or until all players have hit in the long game (explained later)

Scoring, Golchery Putting

- A ball which rolls through the opening, and hits the back brace, is 3 points.
- A ball which rolls through the opening, stopping short of the line 10 feet beyond the buh, is 2 points. (To be through the opening, the *entire ball* must go through).
- A ball which hits one of the legs, or any other part of the buh, is 1 point.

THE GURU IN YOUR GOLF SWING

Scoring, Golchery Chipping

- A ball which goes through the bulls-eye circle is 3 points.
- A ball which hits any part of the buh is 2 points.
- A ball which rolls through the opening is 1 point. Hitting the back brace, or rolling past the line behind the buh do not apply in chipping.

Determining a Winner: Fast Game Scoring

- The standard fast game is to 9 points. The first team to reach 9 is the winner.
- If only two teams competing, the winner is best 2 of 3 games.
- If more than 2 teams, then time permitting, each team plays each other. The team with the most wins is the victor. If no time to play every team, the team with the most wins is again the victor.
- In case of tie, the winner is the team with the most 3 point shots during the course of play. If that is a tie, each player hits 2 shots from one side. The team with the most points wins. If that is tied, do it again from the other side, etc., until there is a winner.

Determining a Winner: Traditional Game

- Traditional Bhutanese archery rules apply, with some exceptions.
- As before, player one on each team hit 2 balls, alternating shots. The scoring is the same, except that at the end of each series at one buh, the score is only the amount one team scored over the other team's score. For example, if team A scores 5, and team B scores 3, the score after the first series is: team A, 2; team B, 0.
- The first team to 9 is the wins that game. The best 2 of 3 games is the event winner. Unlike the fast game, every player must finish that series, even if a team reaches 9 or above. The reason is, the other team can reduce their opponents score to under 9 with enough hits.

If students seem interested in golf, and/or show unusual aptitude, they are invited to join the ongoing BYGA classes at the Royal Thimphu Golf Club. These are extensive during the winter school break, and include on-course practice on Mondays, as well as ongoing professional instruction. To register a student, and for more information, contact Karma Lam Dorji, Department of Youth and Sports and Bhutan Youth Golf Association: (m): 17111579

APPENDIX 2

YOUTH GOLF SCHEDULE:

Monday: All come at 9:30 to play on course, end at 11:30
Wednesday: Ravens at 9:00 until 10:30
Takins at 10:30 until 12:00
Thursday: Girl Power at 10:00 until 11:30
Friday: All come at 9:30 until 12 (Golchery Tournament)
Team Names
The Girls (3 or 4 on a team):
Ravens
Takins
Girl Power + younger brother
Umma
The Boys:
Tiger
Black hand
4G
Army
Red devil
Beaver
Blackfly
Red Dragon
David Beckham

Jeevan Nidup Tashi (G)
Dip Tendzi Sonam Wangchuck
Bidan Thinley Jigme Tobgay
Tashi Wangdi Shambar Dorji (G)
Rinchen Thinley Tsegyal
Thinley Sangay Mila
Chenadorji Karma Doogie
Tendin Shechep Raju Biswa Rinzin (G)
Sonam Mike Wier Vijay Pem Choki (G)

Wang Rana Dodo Jamyang Choden (G)
Kesang Druk Tashi Wangchu Pema (G)
Kinzang Choki Dorji Yeshey (G)
Sonam Samten Gagyal Dechen
Dechen Ugyen Nin Dorji Ugyen Wenzel
Tashi Namgyal Yosel B. Kalden
Sonam Tshering Mani Kumar Tshering Denma
Sonam Yeshe Arun Pema (G)
*Please only come at your allotted time. 3 unexcused absent; name taken off the list
*Field trip every other Tuesday: 9:30, Internet every other Tuesday, 3:00

APPENDIX 3

Meditation is not:

A religion
A blissful state of mind (although it could be)
'Zoning out'
A blank mind
A waste of time
Goofy
Weird
Cosmic
A 'dream'-state
Doing nothing (scientists are proving the brain is very active)

What you don't have to do

Join a cult
Wear robes
Worship statues
Dance around and give out flowers
Give up fun stuff
Spend more than 20 minutes a day
Pay money
Become a vegetarian
Be different or somebody else
Tell anybody if you don't want to

To study further the meditation presented in this book:
https://shambhala.org/programs/

For a full list of international meditation groups:
Mindful Magazine: https://www.mindful.org
The Lions Roar Magazine: https://www.lionsroar.com/

Apps for meditation:
https://www.headspace.com/
https://www.10percenthappier.com/
https://www.wecroak.com/
https://ca.tm.org/transcendental-meditation-halifax

Sources

Trungpa, Chögyam. *Cutting through Spiritual Materialism*, Shambhala Publications, United States, 1973

Parent, Joseph. *Zen Golf*, Doubleday, New York, 2002

——————— *Zen Putting*, Gotham Books, New York, 2007

Holecek, Andrew, *Dream Yoga*, Sounds True, Boulder Colorado, 2016

Gilbert, Elizabeth. *Big Magic*, Riverhead Books, New York, 2015

Wright, Robert. *Why Buddhism is True*, Simon and Schuster, New York, 2017

Wallace, Alan B. *Dreaming Yourself Awake*, Shambhala Publications, Boston, 2012

Hebron, Michael. *The Art and Zen of Learning Golf*, Learning Golf Inc. Smithtown, New York, 2005

Nilsson and Marriott. *Be a Player*, Atria Books, New York, 2017

Nelson, Byron. *Winning Golf*, Taylor Trade Publishing, New York, 1992

Chödrön, Pema. T*he Places that Scare You*, Shambhala Classics, Boston, 2002

Penick, Harvey. *Little Red Book*, Simon and Schuster, New York, 1992

Mipham, Sakyong. *Turning the Mind into an Ally*, Riverhead Books, New York, 2003

Tendzin, Osel. *Buddha in the Palm of your Hand*, Shambhala, 1982

Wright, Norrie, *The Wright Swing* DVD, Centre Productions

About the author

Ed Hanczaryk is a golf professional, a member of the PGA of America and PGA of Canada. He served his PGA apprenticeship at Lake Valley Golf Club in Boulder, Colorado and Sawgrass Country Club in Ponte Vedra, Florida.

He was named a Top 50 Teacher in Canada by the *National Post* magazine and was voted by his peers as Teacher of the Year in Eastern Canada four years in a row. He currently teaches at The Links at Penn Hills in Nova Scotia in the summer and The Awareness Golf School year-round. (www.awarenessgolf.com)

He has been meditating since 1974.

Knot of eternity.

9 HOLE COURSE

ROYAL THIMPHU GOLF CLUB BHUTAN

LOCAL RULES

The Game of Golf shall be played in accordance to the current **USGA** Rules of Golf and the Local Rules of the **ROYAL THIMPHU GOLF CLUB.**

I. **FREE DROP**
    A ball embedded in its own pitch-mark through the green may be lifted, cleaned and dropped without penalty, as near as possible to the spot where it lay but not nearer to the hole.
    A ball landing in the Nursery area (above the 9th/18th Green) may be dropped without a penalty in the designated area.
    All areas marked as GUR/White Marks.

II. **OUT OF BOUNDS**
    All areas beyond the course fence and the area as designated below are out of bounds:

1st/10th Hole - Right side of the blue stakes one stroke penalty.
2nd/11th Hole - Left side of the blue stakes one stroke penalty.
                - Right side of the blue stakes one stroke penalty.
3rd/12th Hole - Left side of the blue stakes one stroke penalty.
                - Right side of the blue stakes one stroke penalty.
4th/13th Hole - Right side of the blue stakes one stroke penalty.
5th/14th Hole - Left side of the blue stakes one stroke penalty.
6th/15th Hole - Right side of the course fence OB.

7th/16th Hole - Right side of the stone wall fence and the
                - white stakes OB. Left side of the blue
                - stakes one stroke penalty.
8th/17th Hole - Right side of the course fence OB. Left side of
                - blue stakes one stroke penalty.
9th/18th Hole - Right side of the corse fence OB. Left side
                - of the blue stakes and towards the club house
                - one stroke penalty.

III. No equipment other than the putter is permitted on the greens.
IV. Practice is permitted in designated areas only. No putting practices is allowed on the Greens.
V.   Local Rules are subject to change from season to season. New rules and the changes will be put on RTGC notice board.
VI. Water Hazards and Lateral Hazards
     Any ball entering the water / channel must be dropped in the designated area under penalty of one stroke.
     Lateral Hazards are all marked by the **red stakes.** If any player grounds his club grounds it during a practice swing shall be liable to one penalty stroke.
VII. **Priority Rules:** Please repair your divots and pitch-mark on the greens. Avoid slow play.
     RTGC being an open course kindly refrain from any loud applause/noise/shouting during play.
     Do not litter on the course.

Hiking up to Taktsang.